BEAD
EMBROIDERY

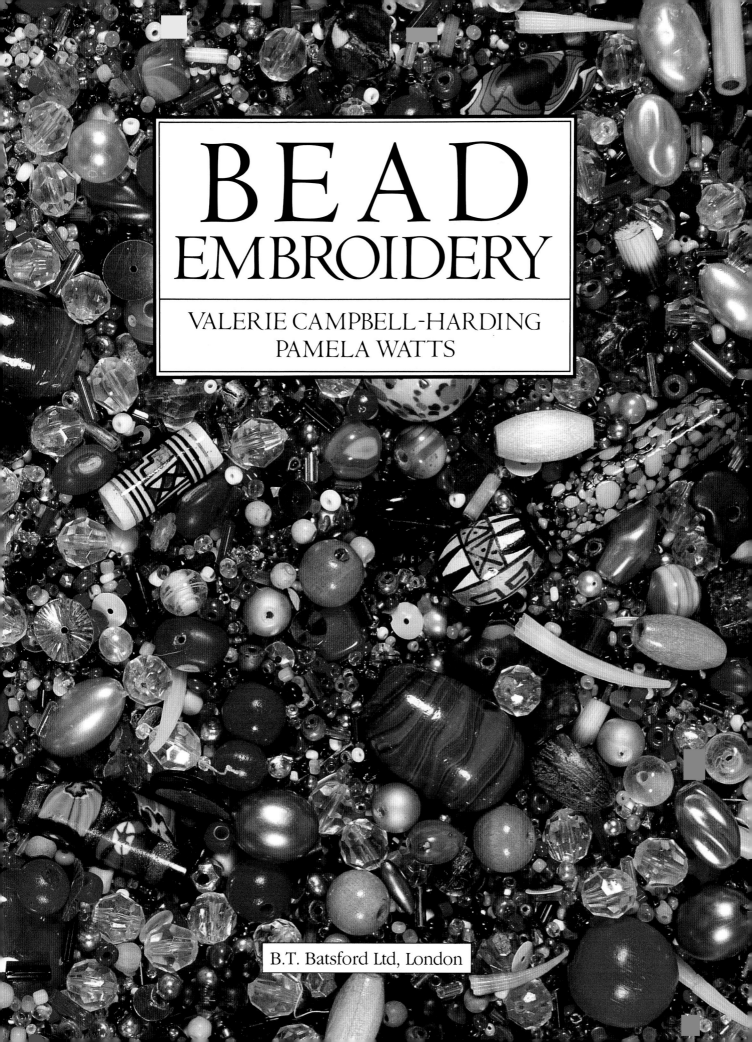

BEAD
EMBROIDERY

VALERIE CAMPBELL-HARDING
PAMELA WATTS

B.T. Batsford Ltd, London

ACKNOWLEDGEMENTS

Very special thanks to our students, colleagues
and friends for allowing us to photograph their
work to illustrate this book. Our thanks to
Peter Reid and David Partridge for taking some
of the photographs and to Christina Barry for
the inspiring fashion drawings. We are grateful
to Pfaff for the loan of sewing machines and to
Offray for providing ribbons.

The embroidery is the work of the authors
unless otherwise stated. The diagrams are
by Valerie Campbell-Harding using a
Macintosh computer.

First published 1993

Reprinted 1994, 1996
Reissued 2000

Typeset by Servis Filmsetting Ltd, Manchester
and printed in Hong Kong

Published by
B.T. Batsford Ltd
9 Blenheim Court
Brewery Road
London N7 9NT

A member of the Chrysalis Group plc

British Library Cataloguing-in-Publication Data.
A catalogue record for this book is available from the
British Library.

ISBN 0 7134 8606 6

JACKET ILLUSTRATION:
*Rich beading using jewels and glass, pearls and silver-
lined beads, some stitched flat on the fabric and some on
stalks. The beading has been painted with glass paint and
pearlized fabric paints*

PAGE 1:
*Embroidered book cover incorporating small squares
and long strips of bead weaving using variegated
metallic beads, blackberries, daisy chains and machine
embroidery, built up in layers to give richness*

PAGES 2–3:
*Some of the many beads and bugles imported from all
over the world and available commercially*

CONTENTS

INTRODUCTION

Beads have been treasured and collected throughout history and in all corners of the world. They have been used as symbols to denote wealth, love and status; as currency to bribe and barter; to ensure health and luck and to ward off evil spirits. How many of us can honestly say that we have ever thrown beads out? Old, broken strings of beads, fragments of fringing and forgotten necklaces are lovingly stored away. We keep little packets, boxes and jars containing beads – all waiting to be used for something.

This book is a practical and, we hope, inspirational guide to using beads with embroidery. After the Second World War, the necessary practice of using whatever materials were available with beads and found objects tarnished the image of using beads for many of today's embroiderers. A glance at the illustrations in this book, however, should dispel any feeling that beads are merely added in a last-ditch attempt to recover a piece of boring work. Here beads are shown as the very essence of the embroidery. The fabrics, techniques and stitches integrate with, support and glorify the use of beads. We show you how to make them, paint them and, above all, how to use them to add richness, shine, colour, texture and weight to your work. Beads can be large or small, round, square or long, matt or shiny, coloured or clear, carved or painted, tarnished and tatty, but their fascination remains.

A complete history of how beads have been made and used over the centuries would fill a separate volume and could be said to be a history of mankind itself. From the earliest tribal body-painting and bead necklaces to Victorian ladies' obsession with beads and the dresses of the 1920s and '30s, the story continues. We hope that the ideas and techniques contained in this book will provide another chapter in the long history of beads.

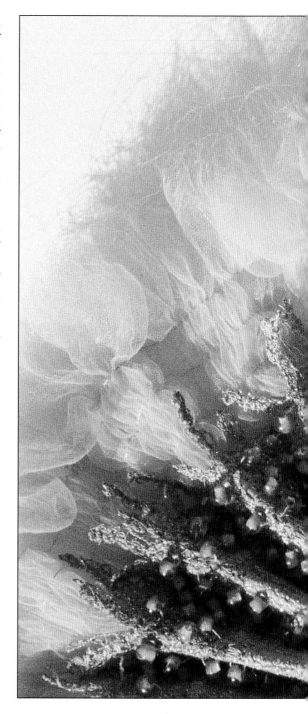

Golden citrine *fan. The
stiff folds encrusted
with beads contrast
with the delicacy of the
gathered chiffon edge*
(Diana Dolman)

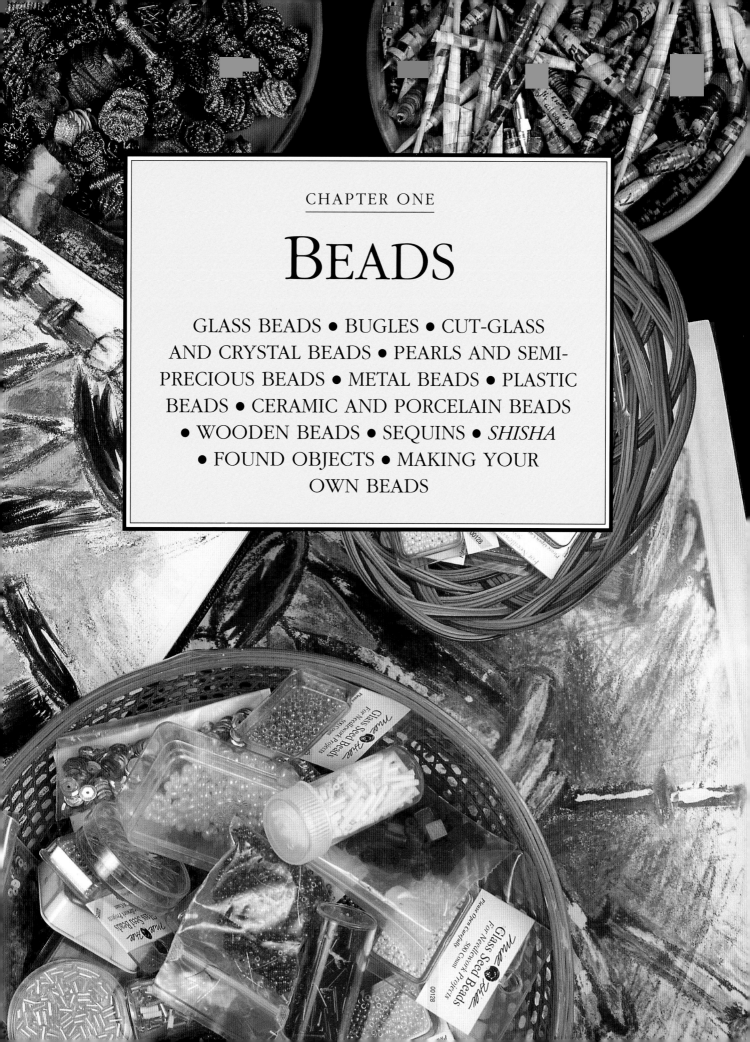

CHAPTER ONE

BEADS

GLASS BEADS • BUGLES • CUT-GLASS
AND CRYSTAL BEADS • PEARLS AND SEMI-
PRECIOUS BEADS • METAL BEADS • PLASTIC
BEADS • CERAMIC AND PORCELAIN BEADS
• WOODEN BEADS • SEQUINS • *SHISHA*
• FOUND OBJECTS • MAKING YOUR
OWN BEADS

(Previous page)
A variety of beads, including home-made paper, fabric and wire beads, commercial beads and bugles, large decorated beads with patterns suitable for designs, a sketchbook showing drawings of large beads and a beadmaking tool

To describe a bead as a round object with a hole through it is far too simple. The fascination lies in the variety of shape, size and colour, the surface texture, what it is made of and all the possible combinations of these and other factors.

The names given to beads can cause confusion, as some are terms used in the trade or have historical or regional origins. Trade beads were an essential item for early white explorers and traders when travelling among primitive tribes. The beads were used as gifts and in exchange for valuable furs, beaver skins, ivory and other commodities.

Using beads as currency may well have influenced the style of embroidery and beadwork of many ethnic cultures. Pony beads – opaque china beads manufactured in Venice – were imported into North America in the early nineteenth century. Mostly black, white, yellow and blue, they were taken to the Plains tribes by pony pack trains, hence their name.

Another term not often used today is 'pound beads'. This refers to the glass beads imported into Britain from Germany and Italy in the nineteenth century. It would appear that the Victorian lady ordered her beads by the pound, rather than the ounce.

The following descriptions are intended as a guide to the beads widely available today.

GLASS BEADS

Small, round, glass beads are often described as seed beads. They vary in size from 5/0 (large) to 24/0 (very small), i.e., the higher the number, the smaller the bead. The most usual sizes range from 8/0 to 10/0 or 11/0. Antique beads are even smaller – sometimes the size of a grain of sand.

Seed beads are normally sold by metric weight, for example in batches of 25 grams, 100 grams or 0·5 kilogram. However, some suppliers offer packets, plastic tubes or beads by the counted 'measure' in quantities of perhaps 250 or 500. 500 beads may sound a great many, but, taking size 10/0 as an example, 500 beads will easily fit on to a teaspoon, so bear this in mind when ordering by post.

The trade name for small, glass beads is rocailles, and this can often be seen in catalogues today. The term rocailles is further divided into round rocailles (smooth on the outside and inside); Tosca or square rocailles (smooth on the outside with a square-cut inside to catch the light); and Charlottes (ridged or faceted on the outside with a square-cut or metal-lined inside).

Apart from the obvious choice of colours available, different surface finishes add to the range. Glass beads may be transparent, opaque, pearly, metallic, iridescent or silver-lined. The metallic finish applied to the outside of glass beads is usually gold, silver, bronze or gunmetal. These, as well as silver-lined beads, may darken with age and wear. Brightly coloured metallic beads are not colourfast.

BUGLES

These are tube-shaped glass beads ranging from 2 mm to approximately 35 mm ($\frac{1}{16}$ to $1\frac{1}{2}$ ins) in length. As with round beads, the surface can be smooth and round or faceted, with the same range of permutations in colour and finish.

Bugles made of jet were very popular in the late nineteenth century for fringes, household items and accessories, and, later, in the 1920s and '30s for dress. Some Indian bugle beads are elaborately painted and twisted like barley-sugar sticks.

The weight of the longer bugles should be taken into consideration as this can wear and fray the thread alarmingly quickly.

CUT-GLASS AND CRYSTAL BEADS

Cut-glass, as the name implies, gives a highly reflective, faceted surface to the beads, which come in a wide variety of sizes, shapes and colours. The larger shapes, such as pendants, drops, ovals and heart shapes, have a hole at one end. They are more commonly associated with jewellery than with embroidery, as are the square and rectangular shapes set in metal mounts.

(Above)
Small picture using dyed and painted beads, purls, bugles, discs and star shapes
(Yvonne Morton)

(Opposite)
Richly embroidered vessel with a pool of beads and padded leather shapes to give the effect of molten metal
(Penny Burnfield)

Peaked cap using couched and stitched bugles, showing a design of balloons
(Caroline Page)

PLASTIC BEADS

When compared to glass, semi-precious stone, wood or ceramic, the term 'plastic bead' has an unfortunate ring to it. Due to modern methods of manufacture, however, some plastic beads are actually quite attractive, with the advantage of being lighter in weight than many other beads. They are available in a wide range of sizes and shapes – round, square or cubed – with a smooth or faceted surface.

As well as being made in a range of colours, plastic beads can be transparent, translucent, gold or silver and, perhaps most usefully, some have a matt, opaque finish which has a slightly luminous quality. These would contrast well with beads of other substances, adding a different surface texture in a piece of embroidery.

CERAMIC AND PORCELAIN BEADS

Most people are tempted at some time to buy ceramic beads. They are normally fairly large and heavy, often with very attractive and intricate hand-painted patterns and designs. These beads need to be used with care as their size and visual weight can dominate a piece of work. They can, however, be used to good effect in making tassels with elaborate heads, as the large central hole takes cords or bundles of thread easily.

WOODEN BEADS

These are often thought of as ethnic in character and, like ceramic beads, can be a tempting purchase. As well as having a natural finish, many wooden beads are polished, varnished, stained, carved or painted. They come in the usual range of sizes and shapes and are relatively light in weight.

PEARLS AND SEMI-PRECIOUS BEADS

As products of nature, these beads have special qualities and are prized for their uniqueness. Round beads of various sizes are available in pearl, amethyst, coral, agate, quartz, tiger's eye and many other semi-precious stones. Especially attractive for embroidery (and much cheaper) are the 'chips' of irregular, odd shapes, as well as freshwater and blister pearls.

METAL BEADS

As well as the metallic finish applied to glass, beads can be made of metal. Sterling-silver and nine-carat-gold beads are usually 2 mm ($\frac{1}{16}$ in) in size and are sold singly. They are used to add a very special touch to a piece of embroidery.

Other metal beads are also available, such as brass, steel (which rusts in a damp atmosphere), or aluminium, which is a rather harsh, bright-silver colour.

SEQUINS

Sequins and spangles are known in the trade as paillettes. These shiny shapes of thin metal or plastic are generally all referred to as sequins, whereas, in fact, sequins have a hole at one side and spangles have a hole in the centre.

As well as the familiar circles, sequins are also available as ovals, squares and in a multitude of novelty shapes in metallic, pearlized or iridescent colours. Spangles are sometimes indented into a cup shape, which is flat in the centre with a raised edge, known as a couvette. Spangles and sequins have been used in the Far East and Europe for many centuries, coming into prominence in this country during the nineteenth and twentieth centuries for dress and accessories.

SHISHA

Traditionally associated with Indian and Pakistani embroidery, *shisha* are pieces of mica or mirror glass which are applied to fabric. They are usually slightly irregular round shapes, but can also be square, triangular or oblong and come in a variety of sizes. The colour also varies from the reflective mirror-glass colour to gold, green or blue.

FOUND OBJECTS

Almost anything could fall into this category with the great proviso that, whatever you use, it should be an essential element in the design and not a gimmick. Over the years and in certain parts of the world, beetle wings, shells, buttons, pebbles, quills and seeds have all been used for bead embroidery.

Seeds need to be pierced with a hole while they are still fresh, although if they are already hard, a

Detail of a panel using dyed and painted pleated fabrics with dyed pearls
(Diana Dolman)

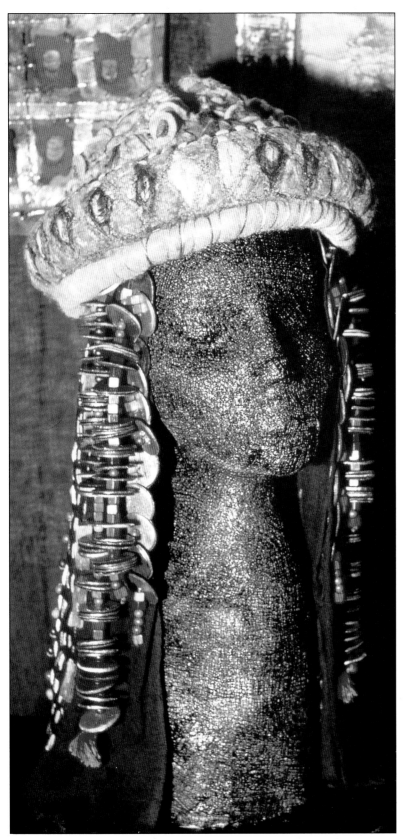

red-hot needle will usually work without causing cracking. Dyeing or painting the seeds will often integrate them into the work more successfully.

This also applies to slices of polythene tubing or short lengths of drinking straws. Curtain rings and washers may be painted or wrapped with thread before being stitched to fabric.

MAKING YOUR OWN BEADS

From the variety listed so far, it may seem unnecessary to want to make your own beads. It is very satisfying, on the other hand, to know that you have been in control of every aspect of your work. We hope that some of the methods described on pages 16 and 17 will inspire some really original, unique beads. We are not including instructions for the proprietary clay-moulded beads normally sold as kits for children.

(Opposite, left)
*Embroidered hat,
including cut-through
appliqué and machine
embroidery with
strung beads and discs
hanging from each
side* (Joan Powell)

(Opposite, right)
*Detail of the beads
showing painted Fimo
discs and round and
square wooden beads*
(Joan Powell)

*A large hanging
showing a North
American Indian in
bas relief in machine
embroidery and beads*
(Frances Manz). *A
detail of the hanging
can be seen overleaf*

shape and light enough to be rolled without tearing or creasing. Typing paper, gift-wrap, magazines, catalogues and newspaper are all suitable. The only equipment needed is thick wire or a fine, metal knitting needle and paper adhesive.

With a little skill and ingenuity, it is possible to create a special rolled-paper-bead maker, as shown in the photograph on page 23. Choose one of the patterns from the diagram opposite, remembering that the length of the strip will determine how fat the bead will be, and the width of the strip how long the bead will be.

Starting with the wide end, roll the paper firmly and evenly round the wire or knitting needle. When about two-thirds has been rolled, spread adhesive along the remainder of the strip and roll to the end. Make sure that the tip is well-secured with adhesive before leaving to dry. Gently twist the bead off the needle. When dry, paper beads can be painted or streaked with extra colour, or varnished or waxed for a more durable finish.

Fabric beads

The same technique used for rolled-paper beads can be adapted to make fabric beads. Choose a material which is reasonably firm and closely woven. (The cut side edges of a loosely woven fabric strip would fray too much, although the adhesive does help to prevent this.) Wind the strip of fabric very tightly round the wire or knitting needle, applying a light film of fabric adhesive as you go. Make sure that the end tip of the fabric is well-secured before leaving to dry.

The fabric for the beads may be printed, painted or dyed at the same time as the fabrics for the embroidery. Alternatively, the dry beads can be painted using fabric paint in a mixture of colour streaks, or one of the lovely metallic fabric paints.

A detail of the Indian showing the fringe on the sleeve, which includes rolled-fabric beads and gold-painted shells strung with small rocailles (Frances Manz)

Paper beads

Rolled-up strips of paper make fascinating and inexpensive beads. If part of your design work has included printing and painting on paper, then try using the same paper to make the beads for inclusion with the embroidery. Use any good-quality paper which is heavy enough to hold its

Rose-petal beads

Pulped rose-petal beads were popular in Victorian times. Use fresh petals of dark red, perfumed roses for the best results. Place the petals in a food processor or blender until they resemble a smooth pulp. Refrigerate for twenty-four hours. Mould and roll the pulp into bead shapes, moistening it a little if the pulp crumbles. Make the beads at least twice as large as you require as they will shrink while drying.

Before the beads are completely dry, pierce the hole with a large hat pin. The surface can be decorated with a craft knife or pitted with the point of a knitting needle. Polish with a piece of velvet or paint with clear varnish when dry. If left unvarnished, the rose petals will retain their perfume.

An even more interesting use of rose petals for beads is connected with the Roman Catholic rosary, which consists of 165 beads used to count the 150 Aves and the 15 Paternosters and Glorias. Originally the beads were made from carefully rolled-up rose petals, sometimes darkened with lampblack to preserve them. This must account for the origins of the name rosary given to the string of prayer beads. Adapting the rolled-paper-bead technique and making your own beads from petals would make a fascinating summer project.

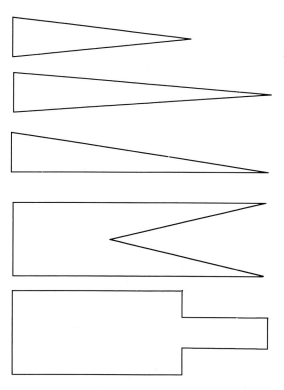

Some of the shapes which may be cut from papers or fabrics to make rolled beads

Sealing-wax beads

Light a candle, making sure that you are working away from draughts. Take some thick wire or a fine knitting needle, and hold this and the sealing wax above the flame. As the wax melts on to the wire, roll it round and round to make a bead.

Experiment by mixing colours together, add gold or coloured streaks, or push tiny beads, scraps of thread or glitter into the soft wax. Lay the wire over the top of a bowl or jam jar to harden. Heat the wire carefully on each side of the bead before slipping it off.

Bonded-fabric beads

A method of making attractive and durable fabric beads is to use Vilene Bondaweb instead of ordinary adhesive. Iron Bondaweb on to the back of fine silk fabric, leaving the protective paper in place. Draw the first of the pattern shapes shown above on to the fabric, and cut it out.

Place a candle on a protective mat, making sure that there are no draughts. Touch the sides of the fabric shape into the candle flame, a little at a time, extinguishing any remaining flame with an old rag. This seals, singes and colours the edges. Remove the paper backing.

While it is still warm, roll the fabric tightly round a piece of firm wire or a thin knitting needle. Before slipping the bead off the wire, roll

it lightly on to the surface of a hot iron to secure the tip.

Wire beads

Wind fine wire, fuse wire or plastic-coated telephone or computer wire round a thick sewing needle to make a small bead. Wrap it over and over on top of itself to build up the shape. Using your sewing machine, try zigzagging over the wire with a metallic thread before wrapping it round the needle, to give a more textured bead.

To make a larger bead, bend the end of the wire over to make a hook, and thread it into a length of tubular knitting ribbon yarn. Zigzag over the two together, wrapping to make a bead as described above.

The rayon yarn takes dye beautifully, and is also now available in shaded and variegated colours. Interesting effects can be achieved by working an open zigzag stitch with a toning or contrasting colour of thread in the machine.

A pair of tweezers is useful to tuck in the wire ends before slipping the bead off the needle.

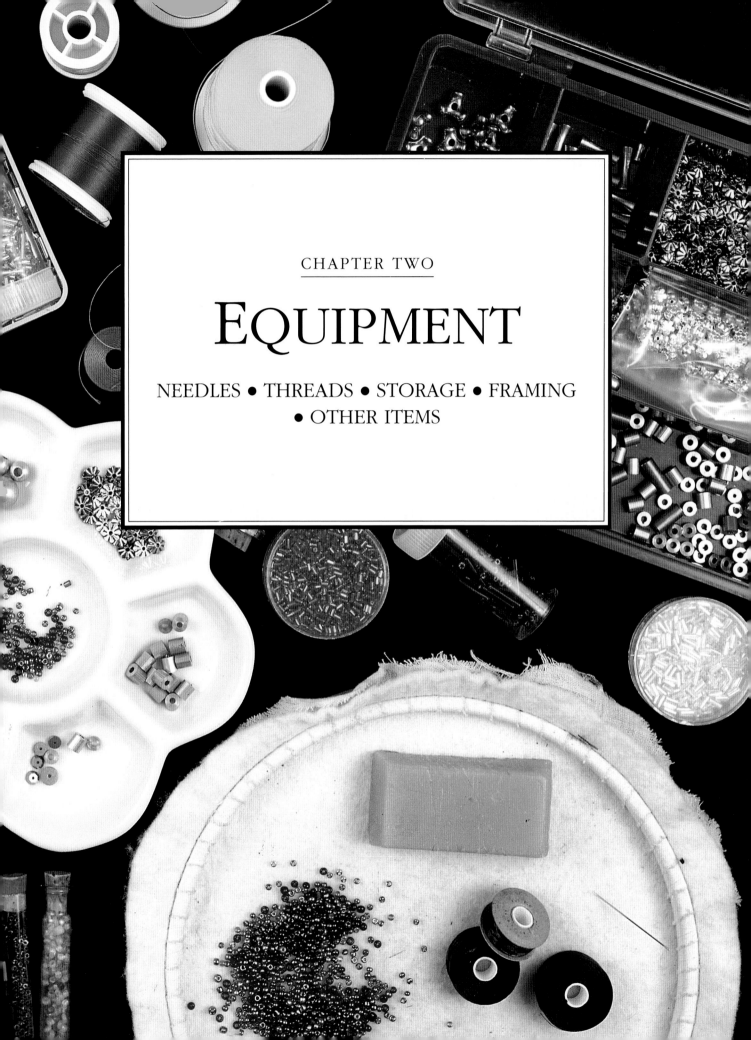

CHAPTER TWO

EQUIPMENT

NEEDLES • THREADS • STORAGE • FRAMING
• OTHER ITEMS

Specialized, expensive equipment is not necessary for the majority of beadwork techniques, but there are some items that you will find useful. Having the right thread, needles and method of storing your beads can make the work easier and more pleasant to do.

NEEDLES

The type and size of needle that you use obviously depends on the size of the hole in the bead and, to some extent, on the technique and preference of the worker. The size-numbering system for needles is the same as for beads – the higher the number, the smaller the needle.

For many beads, a betweens or quilting needle, size 10, will be suitable. This is a short needle with a small rounded eye which should pass through a size 10/0 bead. If you prefer a longer needle, use a Sharps needle, size 10, 11 or 12, again with a small rounded eye, for beads of sizes 10/0 and 11/0.

In general, the size of the needle relates to the size of the bead, number-wise. Beading needles are even longer and finer than the Sharps needles. They are available in sizes 10, 12, 13 and 15, and are used for the smaller-holed beads. The fact that they bend easily can be used to advantage for picking up beads on to the needle, but there comes a point when they actually snap, so do keep plenty in store.

Stringing very small beads on to a thread for couching can be done using a home-made wire 'needle'. Use a 7·5 cm (3 in) length of three- or five-amp fuse wire, doubled over, and put the thread through the looped end. Trim the two ends of the wire to an even length, pushing them together through the hole in the bead. Historically, this was done using a single human hair, which must have been a very tedious process.

Getting the thread through the very fine eye of a beading needle can be a problem. Always cut the end of the thread at an angle, moisten it, then flatten it either with your teeth or a pair of tweezers. Hold it between your thumb and first finger with a very short amount of the thread protruding. If this fails, try a magnifying glass or a needle threader. The latter is often part of the accessories supplied with your sewing machine.

THREADS

When choosing threads, you need to take into account the size of the bead hole and needle eye and the technique to be used, as well as the colour scheme, design and fabric. The basic requirements are that the thread is strong, flexible, knots easily and is resistant to the fraying which results from the friction of the hard bead surface with the thread.

Use the heaviest thread you can get through the needle eye and bead hole, remembering that in some beadwork techniques (such as fringing), the thread needs to pass through the bead twice. Whatever the thread, run it through beeswax or a candle before use as this strengthens it, minimizes fraying and makes the thread more flexible in use.

Fine, synthetic sewing threads such as Drima and Gutermann are strong and excellent for sewing beads on to fabric. Nymo, available from the USA, is similar. Clear or smoke-coloured nylon thread is strong but difficult to use and even more difficult to knot, although it can be used for warping bead looms (see pages 100–1). Fine silk thread is strong and available in a wonderful range of colours. Button thread is also strong but may be too thick for the smaller sizes of needle.

When selecting a thread for sewing on beads it is important to consider the design and purpose of the embroidery, as well as the size of the bead and needle eye. For a practical article or, say, a fringe which will be exposed to hard wear, it is essential to choose the strongest thread possible. For purely decorative effects, choose from the many exciting threads available to embroiderers today. Fine machine-embroidery threads can be used as well as the wide range of metallic, shaded and variegated threads.

Remember that the threads used to secure beads are often a very visible part of the work and can be painted, dyed or space-dyed. Instructions for these techniques can be found in Chapter Three.

STORAGE

Everyone who works with beads seems to devise his or her own system of containers, ranging from antique cabinets, full of little drawers and nostalgia, to workmanlike plastic containers intended for fishermen or DIY enthusiasts.

Look around for little glass bottles or baby-food jars, plastic tubes, pill bottles or discarded

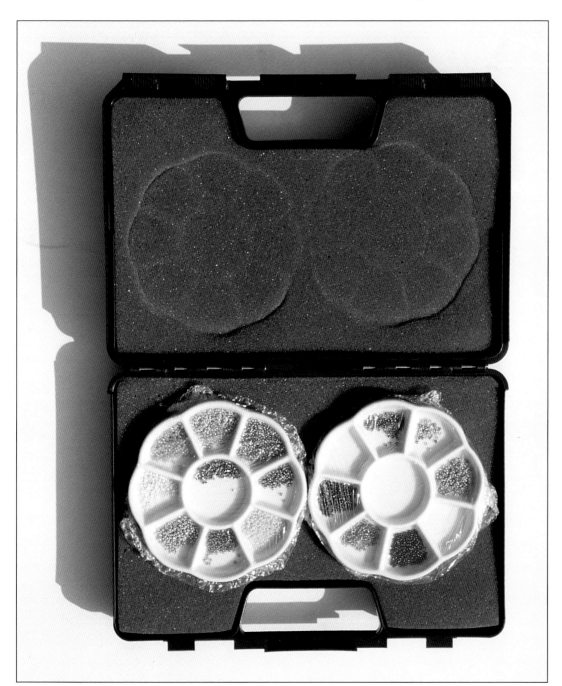

A pistol case used for carrying beads around safely. The ceramic trays holding the beads have a layer of clingfilm over them to stop them sticking to the surface of the foam. The foam is thick enough to prevent the beads from falling out, even when the case is held upside-down

film containers. You may find yourself walking round the supermarket looking for products in containers which could become your bead-storage system. Whatever you choose, remember to keep your beads in the dark as some are prone to fading, especially in sunlight. Never keep beads for long periods in sealed polythene bags.

You will also need some sort of container to use while actually working with the beads. Artists'

white-china watercolour trays are heavy and stable with several separate divisions in which different-coloured beads can be placed. Felt glued on to the bottom of the tray will stop it slipping around. This is a good system if you need to transport your beads to a class or workshop. Stretch cling film over the top and put the tray into a small plastic case with thick pieces of foam in both the lid and base.

A copy of an Edwardian tool originally used for making paper beads. The end of the paper is inserted into the split pin and the handle turned, rolling the bead up tightly, with the paper glued at intervals. We now also use this for making fabric and wire beads

Calico and felt, stretched tightly in a wooden ring frame, works well too. The frame is used upside-down (the opposite way to when working hand embroidery), so that the edges of the frame stop the beads falling off. A tin lid lined with felt works in much the same way, and it is easy to spear the beads with the needle from the felt surface.

Sometimes a flat surface is more convenient when picking up very small beads. Cover a piece of stiff card with a light-coloured nylon velvet. Glue or stitch a piece of felt to the underside. A padded area at one end is useful as a needle- and pin-cushion. This system is often recommended for picking up purls in metal-thread work. The pile of the velvet holds the small beads, enabling you to slip them on to the needle point with ease.

A sugar scoop, rounded or flat-bottomed, or the little plastic scoops supplied with cosmetics, are useful for transferring a quantity of beads from your main storage system to the working container.

FRAMING

It is essential that the fabric is tightly stretched when sewing on beads. For a small piece of work, a wooden ring frame will be suitable; remember to re-tighten the screw from time to time as the work proceeds. It is easier if the frame is supported on a stand, or clamped to a table or arm of a chair, leaving both hands free when working. For larger pieces of embroidery, a slate or square frame will be necessary to take the full size of the design. It is not possible to move a ring frame around once beads have been added to the fabric surface.

In the vast majority of cases, you will need a backing fabric to support the weight of the beads. If choosing calico, make sure that it is light- or medium-weight material, not too closely woven and certainly not heavily dressed. If it is, you will have dreadful trouble getting the very fine needles through it.

OTHER ITEMS

As well as needles, threads, containers, frames and, of course, lots of beads, you will find some, or all, of the following useful.

Pliers

- To cut or form loops in wire
- For pulling a needle that has become stuck through a bead
- To break an unwanted bead in the middle of a row of weaving or couching

Tweezers

- To sort out and pick up very small beads
- To flatten the end of a piece of thread when threading the needle

Bead threader

- A device for rapid threading of beads for couching, comprising a stand and bowl which spins on a pivot. Beads are put in the bowl, and the needle point held amongst them. Spin the bowl and the beads are forced on to the needle.

Polystyrene block

- For making fringes
- For pinning out weaving to finish ends

Graph paper

- For designing complex patterns in fringing and weaving

Magnifying lamp and glass

- For threading needles
- For working with very small beads

Bead loom

- For weaving (can be either home-made or bought)

Stiletto or awl

- To clear a blocked bead hole
- To enlarge the hole in wooden beads

Miscellaneous

- Beeswax for strengthening thread
- Small, sharp embroidery scissors
- Bead varnish or glass paint

CHAPTER THREE

COLOUR

COLOURFASTNESS • BLEACH • PAINTING
BEADS • DYEING PEARLS • PAINTING AND
PRINTING THREADS • GOLD AND SILVER
LEAF • COLOUR EFFECTS • DESIGNING
WITH BEADS

In Zulu beadwork, the language of beads is primarily the language of love.

- White is love that is pure and filled with vision
- Red is more passionate but troubled by feuds and family
- Pink is love threatened by impending poverty
- Yellow is the promise of wealth in marriage
- Green is love pining away as the grass
- Blue is love yearning for flight
- Black is love threatened by anger or jealousy

The deeper meanings are known only to the maker and the person for whom the beadwork is intended. Such feelings are expressed in the colours chosen for chokers, bracelets, coronets, armbands, table-mats and bead sticks.

The connection between colour and the emotions is well known to artists and embroiderers beyond the shores of Africa. The knowledge and practice of colour theory, however, may not be something that is automatically associated with beads or beadwork.

You may think that there are beads of every colour and, indeed, the range of colours is improving, especially in beads from the USA. In fact, beads come in a very limited colour range when compared with fabrics and threads. This is dictated in part by the glass-making process. Glass is coloured with minerals which perform differently depending on the type of glass used for the base and the temperature. Cobalt gives blue; copper gives blue, red, pink or brown; manganese gives violet or brownish-pink; chromium gives green; gold gives pink and red; cadmium give yellow; silver gives amber and selenium gives red and orange. Black is produced by using large amounts of manganese.

As a result of this somewhat limited colour range, it is useful to try out different ways of changing the colour – real or apparent – of the beads, adding your own colours and subtle variations.

COLOURFASTNESS

Only beads coloured all the way through are colourfast. Those with coloured linings or painted surfaces are not, and washing, cleaning and exposure to light will fade the colour after a time. Beads with a metallic finish will darken with age.

BLEACH

The tendency to fade or discolour can be accelerated by the use of bleach. This can be an advantage if you have beads which are too bright or a collection of old and tatty beads in need of rejuvenation. Silver-lined beads can appear garish and bleach will remove the lining. Mix a 50:50 solution of bleach and water in a glass bowl. Add the beads, and leave them to soak for two to three hours. Check them periodically, removing a few beads at various stages in the process. Many painted beads will be restored to their original glass by this method. You can also try acetone instead of bleach. Rinse the beads thoroughly and leave them on kitchen paper to dry naturally.

The beads may appear dull or matt after bleaching. You may choose to leave them like this, but, if you prefer a shiny finish, place the beads on a piece of felt and rub over them with a felt pad or soft tissue.

PAINTING BEADS

French enamel varnish and glass paint are obtainable from many craft shops or by mail order (see the list of suppliers on page 127). The varnish is available in sixteen colours as well as a clear mixing solution to lighten a colour.

Choose white or very pale opaque, satin or lustre beads, transparent or metallic beads or pearls. Bear in mind that the colour may fade

eventually as it is not guaranteed colourfast. Mix one part French enamel varnish to two parts methylated spirits in a jar (do not be tempted to increase the proportion of varnish or the beads will become sticky). This mixture will keep for a few weeks in a jar with a tight-fitting lid.

Small beads need to be strung on to a length of thread before being dipped into the solution, whereas larger beads can be threaded on to wire and painted with a fine paintbrush. Try streaking colour on to larger beads instead of covering the whole area. Whichever method is used, blot excess colour with kitchen paper to prevent patchiness. Leave the beads to dry naturally. Dip or paint again to achieve a darker colour.

The main purpose of painting your own beads is to remove the commercial uniformity, adding those irregularities that are so coveted in ethnic beads. To paint too perfectly is a big mistake. Let the surface be mottled and streaked with colours blending into each other. You will find that beads painted in this way relate much better to the fabric behind them, especially if that has been space-dyed, printed or marbled.

It is great fun to sew the beads on to the fabric, perhaps using beads all of one colour or those colours which you do not like very much, and then to paint the beads with a brush or piece of sponge. Some of the colour will undoubtedly drip on to the fabric too, giving a beautifully blended and original effect.

Paint strings of small beads, larger beads, jewels or *shisha* glass with glass paint diluted with a little white spirit. Again, this can be done either before or after the beads are sewn on to the fabric.

White and glass beads painted with glass paint to blend with the space-dyed threads. The band of colours on the left shows the original paint colours, which have been diluted to give a softer effect on the beads

Painted sunflower seeds (Cassie White)

DYEING PEARLS

Mix 15 ml (one tablespoonful) of powder dye (such as Dylon hot-water dye) with three cups of boiling water. Add the pearls and boil them for five minutes, and then rinse in diluted vinegar to set the colour. Place the pearls in a sieve, rinsing with cold water until it runs clear. Dry naturally on kitchen paper.

You can also experiment with dyeing pearls using the cold-water method, perhaps at the same time as dyeing a batch of fabrics and threads to use in the same piece of embroidery. Make up the solution using Dylon or Procion dye powder, adding the salt and soda solutions as directed. Soak the pearls for two hours before rinsing and drying as before.

A subtle 'antique' effect can be achieved by boiling pearls in a pan with a couple of tea-bags for about ten minutes. Leave in the pan until cold before rinsing.

PAINTING AND PRINTING THREADS

As well as painting, printing and dyeing your own fabrics, these methods can be used to great effect on the threads used in various bead techniques. Heat-fixed silk paint is perhaps the most suitable to use, as it has a thin consistency and produces strong colour. Some types of fabric paint are too thick, clogging the fine threads needed for the smaller beads.

Wrap threads round a bottle or length of thick plastic tubing before painting or sponging on the colour. Blend the colours, letting them run into each other for the maximum random effect. Leave the threads to dry before fixing the paint with a hairdryer. If the threads feel too stiff, wash and rinse them thoroughly. Use transfer paints for nylon and polyester thread. When using transfer paints, wrap the threads round a large piece of card before ironing the painted papers on to each side in turn.

Subtle colour effects can be achieved with the warps on a bead loom when using transparent beads. Either paint the threads first, or add streaks, stripes or blotches of colour to the threads after warping.

In some bead techniques, such as couching, sewing sequins and attaching *shisha*, the thread used becomes a very visible part of the effect. A little time spent in painting the thread will always enhance the finished result.

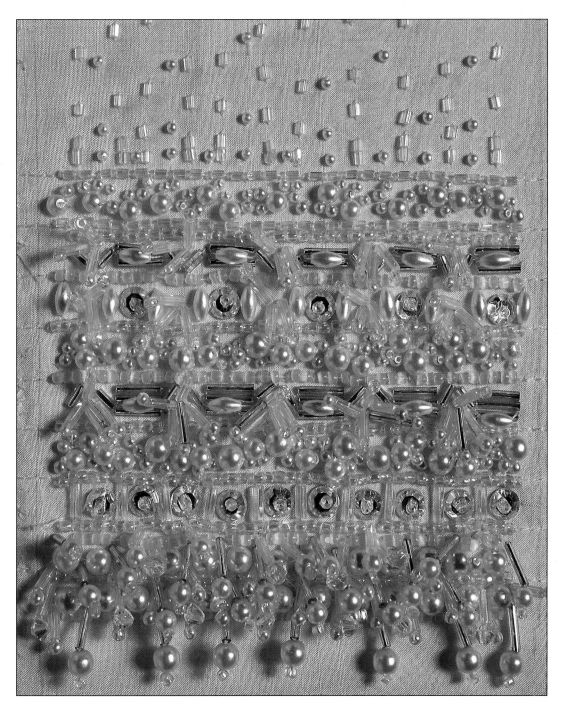

Rich beading using jewels and glass, pearls and silver-lined beads, some stitched flat on the fabric and some on stalks. Overleaf the same sample has been coloured using glass and fabric paints

As an addition or alternative, transfer the gold leaf with Vilene Bondaweb on to areas of the fabric. Add different-coloured transparent beads over the top, allowing the gold to show through to give a subtle gleam to the design.

Here, the beading from the previous page has been painted with glass paint and pearlized fabric paints

(Right)
Suggestion for a wedding dress using the white and pearl sample on the previous page (Christina Barry)

GOLD AND SILVER LEAF

Gold and silver leaf with a paper backing is available (see the list of suppliers on page 127). You can cover areas of large individual beads with this, as well as creating experimental effects on bead weaving and beads sewn on to fabric.

Paint the beads with PVA adhesive and allow to dry (they can be left in this state for any length of time). Moisten very slightly with gin before pressing the transfer leaf on to the beads with a finger. This technique may be used to highlight part of a bead or jewel, or an area of sewn or woven beadwork.

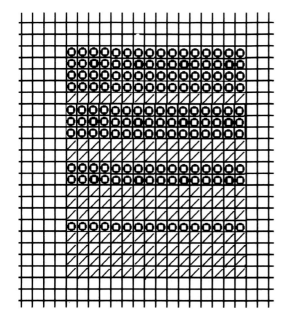

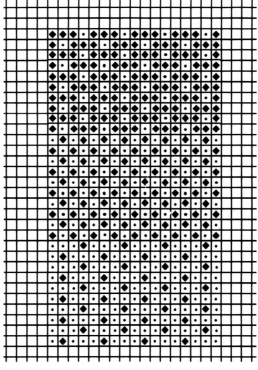

Diagrams showing ways of mixing two colours gradually to avoid a hard line. How well they mix depends on the size of the bead – the smaller the bead, the more the colours will mix

COLOUR EFFECTS

A knowledge of colour theory and the colour wheel will suggest many exciting ways of using beads to give apparent colour changes. Optical mixing, as used by the Impressionist painters, can be achieved using small beads on canvas, areas of hand or machine couching or bead-loom weaving. Work with the primary colours – red, yellow and blue – in either opaque or transparent coloured beads, first in blocks of one solid colour, then in a mixture of two of the primaries. Red and yellow beads, intermixed, will look orange, especially from a distance. Working through all the permutations, including complementary colour, tint, tone and shade, would last a lifetime.

Change the colour surrounding an area of beads, learning how to use this to advantage when planning a colour scheme. An area of red beads surrounded by black beads, stitches or fabric, will look very different from the same red beads surrounded by blue.

Transparent beads, either clear or coloured, always give surprising results. They reflect the colour in other beads and stitches, and change according to the fabric beneath them and the colour of thread passing through them.

Shiny beads in one colour contrast beautifully with the same colour of bead in an opaque, pearly or matt finish. This applies particularly to a chequerboard arrangement of bugles, with the additional tonal change that occurs when the bugles are sewn in different directions.

We hope that some of these ideas will provide inspiration and guidelines for the creation of

White and gold beads painted with glass and metallic paints. The dark beads are highlighted with gold-transfer leaf

Red, blue and yellow beads mixed to extend the colour range. This works best with tiny beads, and does not work at all with large ones

beads contain lines, shapes and patterns which could be used as the source for an embroidery design.

Choose your favourite bead, drawing all or part of it, in a variety of media. Bold brushstrokes of colour, charcoal or pastel, or a fine line drawing could be the starting point. Look carefully at the way the light is reflected on the surface, and at the shadow a bead makes on the background. Make photocopies of your drawings, cut out areas, overlap and reassemble them until you are happy with the result. This may not look at all like a bead, but is a design to be carried out in embroidery with, of course, beads.

Take a colour scheme for an embroidery from a single precious ceramic or ethnic bead. Observe the exact tint, tone and shade of colour, recording these in paint, crayon or with threads. Semi-precious beads show particularly beautiful colour combinations. Record and use the subtle colours of amethyst, malachite, turquoise or corals.

A selection of beads, strings of beads or pearls, sequins and *shisha* can be photocopied, giving an instant abstract design. Put a sheet of clear acetate on the photocopier, and place the beads on it at random. Add sheer ribbons, threads or fragments of fabric. Cover with a piece of white paper before making the copy. This could then be painted in parts, cut, torn, woven and rearranged until you are happy with the composition.

exciting colour effects using beads. Never think that you just have red beads or green beads – imagine what you could do with them.

DESIGNING WITH BEADS

As well as using beads to interpret a design, they can provide the initial inspiration too. Many of the intricately painted ceramic and carved wooden

(Right)
Mixing different colours on the diagonal

(Far right)
Random colour mixing. This technique is best used together with more solid areas of colour

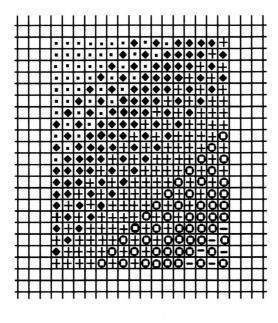

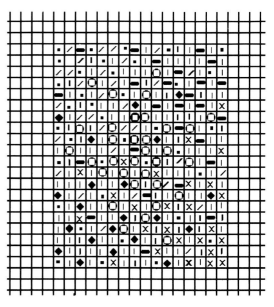

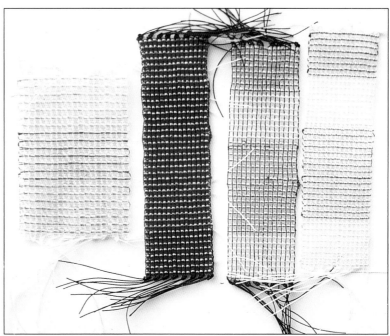

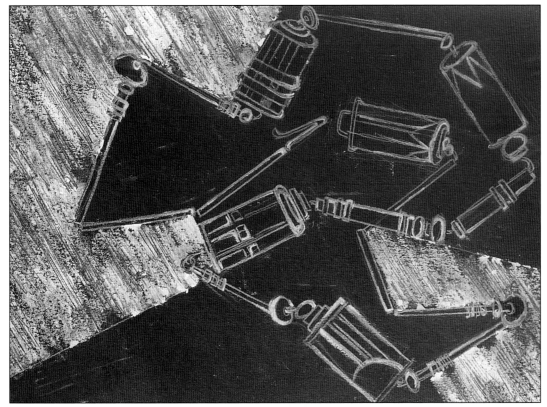

(Above left)
Felt-pen drawings of patterns on beads from India and Peru (Brenda Parsons)

(Above right)
Transparent beads with coloured threads showing through them. The red-glass beads are hardly affected, but the clear-glass beads show subtle effects

(Left)
Drawing of large beads in white chalk on black paper. The background has been coloured and textured in areas using irisé crayons scratched with a knife. This suggests beading, combined with linear embroidery

CHAPTER FOUR

SEWING BEADS

ROUND BEADS • BUGLES • CRYSTAL BEADS
AND JEWELS • SEQUINS • *SHISHA* • DISCS
AND FOUND OBJECTS • COMBINING AND
REPLACING STITCHES WITH BEADS

The exciting part of bead embroidery is that there are as many ways of sewing beads down as there are types of beads – probably more. With a little experience, you will soon devise your own special ways of attaching beads. Use the following suggestions as starting points.

ROUND BEADS

Frame a piece of fabric with a firm backing fabric beneath it in a wooden ring frame. Make sure that it is tightly stretched. A patterned, striped, printed or space-dyed fabric will give you some idea of where to stitch the beads, whereas an expanse of plain fabric can be quite daunting.

Scoop up some different-sized round beads and put them into your working container, or on your lined tin lid, ring frame or velvet-covered pad (see page 22). Cut approximately 45 cm (18 ins) of thread, pull it through beeswax, thread an appropriate needle and make a firm knot at one end. When starting to sew, always take a couple of backstitches into the fabric for extra security. If the bead is fairly large, pick it up between finger and thumb, roll it round so that the hole shows and insert the needle. For small beads it is easier to spear the bead with the needle point from a flat surface. Slide the bead down the thread on to the fabric surface, taking the needle back into the fabric close to the bead.

Continue to sew single beads in this way, some small, some larger, remembering that a cluster or close line of beads will look better than odd ones dotted around. Simple or complex patterns can be arranged as shown in the diagrams on pages 40–1. As you sew every few beads, take a backstitch into the fabric to strengthen the work.

*Sampler showing
many different ways of
sewing on beads and
bugles*

Mirror frame with painted and pleated fabric and mirror, machine embroidery, beads and pearls (Delia Pusey)

(a) and (b) Sewing a single bead to fabric, and (c) sewing on two beads at a time

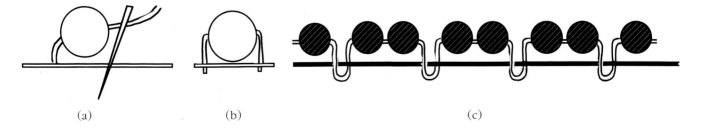

(a)   (b)   (c)

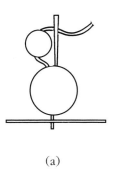

(a)

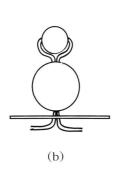

(b)

(c)

(Above)
Sewing two or more beads to fabric to make a 'stalk'

(Right)
Suggestion for a shirt with beads sewn to the stripes in a woven fabric, or next to pintucks (Christina Barry)

(Below)
Detail of a belt in blue satin, with machine embroidery and richly clustered beads (Sue Aubertin)

Little stalks of beads may be made by taking a larger bead on to the thread, then passing it through a smaller one. Take the working thread back through the hole in the larger bead, then into the fabric. Pick up two or three (up to a maximum of eight) beads together on the needle. With the beads on a flat surface, push them up the needle with your left forefinger, holding them on the needle with your right finger. Slide them down the thread. Judge the length of stitch required to equal the length of the beads. This resembles a bullion knot and is known as lazy stitch in American Indian beadwork.

With a number of beads on the thread, try taking the needle back in, or near, the same place from which it emerged, giving a dangling loop of beads. Again, take a number of beads on to the thread but, before entering the fabric, and missing the last bead, run the needle back through the other beads, and then into the fabric.

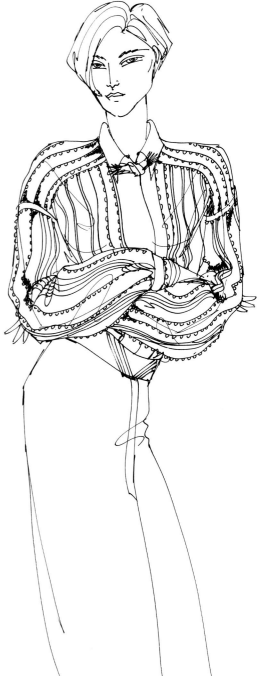

This gives a loose string of beads, as in fringing, which is very effective if several different lengths are worked together in an area. It is possible to create many variations of these strings and stalks by using different sizes, colours and textures of beads.

BUGLES

Long, thin bugle beads add a different element of interest to bead patterns. They can be sewn on individually, as for round beads. After securing the thread with a couple of backstitches, take the needle through the bugle, sliding it down on to the thread. Place in the desired position on the fabric, and then take the thread down close to the end of the bugle. This ensures that it lies firmly and correctly.

You can devise many geometric brick patterns, using different colours or, for a more subtle effect, try the same colour but in a combination of matt, opaque and shiny bugles. Stepped patterns of bugles can form strong design lines in a piece of work, as well as combining beautifully in round and square bead patterns.

Add a small round bead at one or both ends of a bugle, or alternate small round beads sewn together in a line with a bugle of the same length.

Bugles can be made to stand on end on the surface of the fabric, or to protrude over the edge. Take the thread through the bugle, through a small round bead, then back through the bugle before going down into the fabric. One such bugle on its own can look rather strange, so do work a group together, varying the lengths of the bugles and adding one or more round beads on the end.

Painted Russia braid, coiled and stitched to a painted fabric, with knotted and frayed ends. Faceted and glass beads are strung on pink thread to hang loosely (Jill Izzard)

*Patterns combining
round, oval and
square beads, bugles
and sequins or discs*

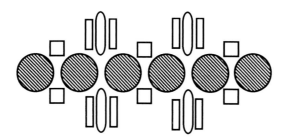

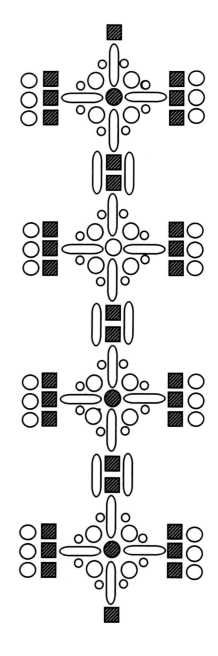

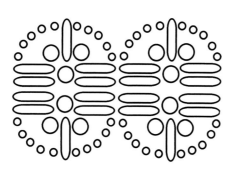

*Three-dimensional
effects using sequins
and beads. Cup
sequins may be laid
front to front or back
to back to raise them,
either parallel to the
fabric or at right
angles to it. A bead
sewn between the
sequins separates them
even more*

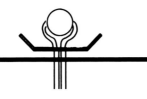

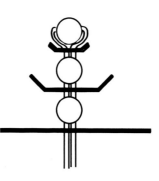

Patterns using bugles, the change of direction giving tonal changes

The common shapes of jewels, showing the stitching holes

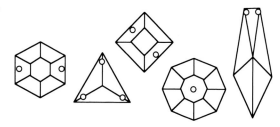

CRYSTAL BEADS AND JEWELS

The larger crystal beads, drops and pendant shapes can be sewn to fabric with the addition of smaller round beads, which helps to prevent the thread fraying on the crystal edge. Using a strong, waxed thread, bring it up through the fabric, through the crystal bead, and then through the smaller bead. Take the thread back through the hole in the crystal before re-entering the fabric. This will look neater than leaving the thread showing at the sides of the large bead.

Methods of sewing on jewels with one, two and four holes

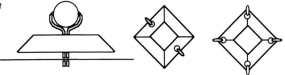

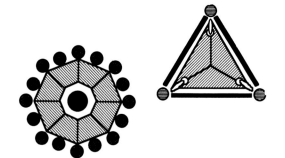

Pendants and drops have one or more holes at one end or around the shape. These holes can appear fairly large, and often look better with a small round bead added in the sewing-on process, as described above.

Added decoration using beads or bugles gives more interest, as do small pieces of fabric, ribbon or braid placed under the jewel

Detail of a belt, showing a richly embroidered ram's head used as a fastening, massed rocailles, and bugles and larger faceted beads supporting the stitched texture and adding highlights (Elsie Probert)

SEQUINS

Sequins may be sewn to fabric singly, in rows, overlapping in rows, upside-down, with decorative stitching and, of course, with added beads and bugles. Choose the thread with care, as it remains visible in the majority of sewing methods. Metal threads look attractive, as do several strands of fine machine-embroidery thread used together, either shaded, variegated or in different colours. Wax the thread as before for ease of sewing and added strength.

Bring the needle up at the edge of a sequin and take it down through the hole, making two, three, four or more stitches radiating around it. Always come up at the edge and go down into the sequin hole for a neater effect. Rows of sequins just touching should be sewn with a long backstitch. For an overlapping row, sew on the first sequin with a backstitch. Pick up the next sequin and make a backstitch in the fabric to the left of the first, so that the second sequin overlaps the first, almost covering the central hole (it takes a little practice to get the spacing exactly right).

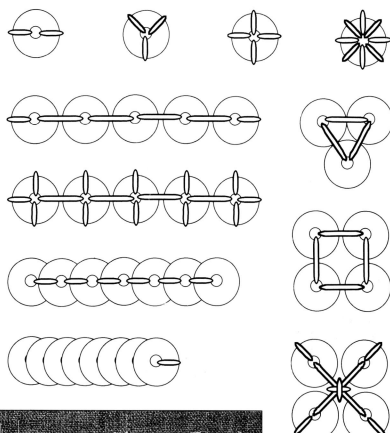

(Above)
Various methods of sewing sequins to fabric. These can be decorative, using a thread of a contrasting colour or texture, or invisible (as shown at the bottom left), when each sequin hides the stitching of the previous one

Detail of a sampler showing some of the sequin shapes available and ways of sewing them to a fabric

The cup- or bowl-shaped sequins are better sewn on with a small bead in the centre. Bring the thread up in the hole, take it through the bead and back through the sequin hole. A bead can be used in this way for attaching flat sequins, too, or a bowl shape, plus bead, over a larger flat sequin.

Experiment with attaching bowl or cup sequins the wrong way up. You could use a pattern of radiating stitches, either evenly spaced or massed over part of the sequin and sparse in others. The stitches can be close to the edge or longer.

Machine-stitched sequins

Many flat sequins are made of thin plastic, enabling a machine stitch to go through them. Test the sequins that you intend to use first, by pushing a hand needle or pin into them to check that they are soft enough. Use a fairly heavy machine needle for sewing. With practice, it is possible to scatter sequins on to a fabric and machine lines of stitching at random over and through them, either with a normal presser foot

or as free machine embroidery. The sequins may well move around in the process, giving a certain freedom to the work, or you can quickly position them on the fabric with a few handstitches first (this is probably safer if you are a little nervous or require a precise pattern). Handstitching first also helps to prevent the sequin rising on to the machine needle when free stitching. If this happens, carefully use a fingernail or stiletto to return the sequin to the fabric, stitching very slowly. An alternative and easier method is to cover the sequins with sheer fabric, torn strips of net or organza before stitching over them, or with cold-water-soluble fabric, which is removed by holding the embroidery under a tap or by using a thick wet brush.

The great attraction of stitching through the sequins in this way is that the massed lines subdue the sometimes garish colour, distort the shapes and break the hard outline of the circles, yet retain the glimmer and shine in a broken pattern. There are many novelty sequin shapes, as well as sequin waste. One possibility might be to cover these with sheer fabric before stitching all over them.

Detail of a panel, showing the contrast of delicate fabrics and massed beads (Sue Aubertin)

SHISHA

As there are no holes in these pieces of mica or mirror glass, they must be attached to the fabric by a network of threads. This exposes the middle part of the *shisha*, while the edges are covered with stitches.

Use a strong waxed thread for the holding stitches, following the diagrams on the right for the sequence and placement of these. With a new decorative thread, work over this framework and down into the surrounding fabric with either cretan, buttonhole or free straight stitches. As you work, the holding stitches will be pulled out to the sides, enlarging the visible central area of the glass. Do not pull too tightly, as the *shisha* has a nasty tendency to pop out at the last moment.

Try placing torn strips of sheer fabric or net over the *shisha* to hold it on to the fabric. Add decorative stitches and beads to secure the fabric strips and *shisha*, and to add decoration.

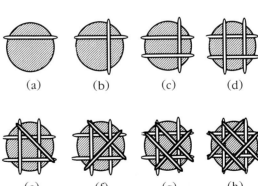

(a) (b) (c) (d)

(e) (f) (g) (h)

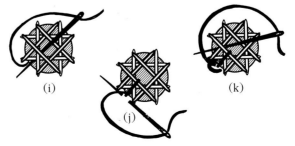

(i) (j) (k) (l)

(Above)
Detail of a panel, using similar shapes and colours but richer fabrics and sparsely placed beads to add colour and shine
(Jan Hay)

The basic method of sewing on shisha *to hold it securely and to cover the sharp edges*

45

DISCS AND FOUND OBJECTS

Many 'found' objects, such as slices of stone, pebbles and pieces of bark or wood cannot easily have holes pierced through them, so use the methods described on the previous page for attaching *shisha*.

Discs, curtain rings and washers can be sewn down as shown in the diagram on the left, with added clusters of beads. The rings can, in many cases, be painted first with glass paint or varnish, or wrapped with fine thread. The main criterion with all such found objects is that they form an integral part of the design and are not just added as a gimmick or afterthought.

COMBINING AND REPLACING STITCHES WITH BEADS

Most embroiderers who love clusters of French knots will have thought of adding beads in amongst them. Try small matt-surface beads with shiny threads, or vice versa. Clear beads will reflect the colours of the surrounding knots. Bullion knots and bugles have an affinity: the colours used can be very similar and subtle, leaving the different textures of the bead and the knot to provide the interest. Massed, freely-worked cross stitch or seeding also acts as a good foil to beads.

Simple composite handstitches (those worked in two separate parts) can be enlivened by the addition of beads. Laced running stitch or Pekinese stitch are good examples. Work a line of

Rings may be secured with small stitches, and small beads added to provide contrast

(Below)
A random effect using laid threads and long ribbons, with beads and bugles to secure them

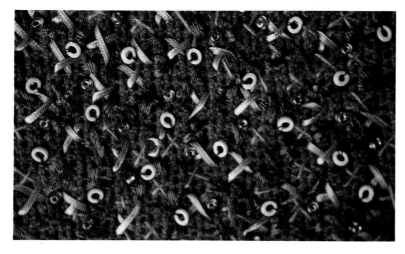

(Above) *Massed cross stitches with green glass beads and tiny discs* (Sarah Wiggs)

Laidwork can include beads sewn on instead of the final stitch to secure the long threads

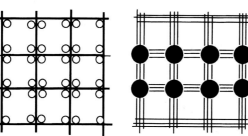

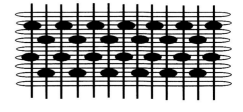

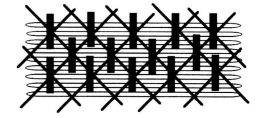

running or backstitch by hand or machine. Lace over or through these with a new thread, picking up a bead with each interlacing stitch.

Laidwork techniques offer many possibilities. Work the basis of the long laid stitches, securing these at intervals with a bead. These can be very precise, traditional patterns or worked to give an entirely free, random effect. Include lengths of thin ribbon, ribbon yarn, machine-wrapped cords or textured threads for extra interest.

Detail of a bag shown on page 34, with felt and fabric shapes surrounded by massed machine stitching and glass, wooden and metallic beads
(Hilary Bower)

COUCHED BEADS

HAND COUCHING • MACHINE COUCHING

In couching, beads are first strung on to a thread or fine wire and then, with a separate thread, stitches are made between the beads to secure the thread to the fabric. There are many variations of bead couching, often associated with ethnic embroidery. In some cases it is difficult to distinguish close lines of couched beads from bead weaving, the latter also having ethnic origins.

Couching was almost certainly devised as a quick way of sewing beads. The ceremonial crowns made by the Yoruba tribe from Benin in Nigeria are complex colour patterns of beads, which completely cover the base fabric. The North American Indians called their method of couching 'lazy squaw stitch' – now known as just lazy stitch – which speaks for itself.

The front of a bag made by North American Cree Indians using couched beads

HAND COUCHING

To decide on the best method of couching, consider the design, the number and size of the beads to be used and whether the beads alone form the decoration. In some cases, one or both of the threads play a part in the overall effect.

Thread a fine needle with strong cotton, working one or two backstitches at the start of the line. Pick up as many beads as required and lay them along the design line. Take the thread down through the fabric at the end of the line to fasten off. Include beads of different sizes and bugles. With a separate thread, work a stitch between each bead to secure the thread to the fabric. In some cases, especially with small beads, it is only necessary to make a holding stitch every two or three beads. The beads can be closely packed along the entire length or spaced out, evenly or in random groups.

A quick method of couching a reasonably short, straight line of beads is to use the same thread for stringing and securing. Fasten the thread on, pick up the beads and take the needle to the back at the end of the line, making a backstitch. Bring the same thread up again, working back along the line with stitches between the beads.

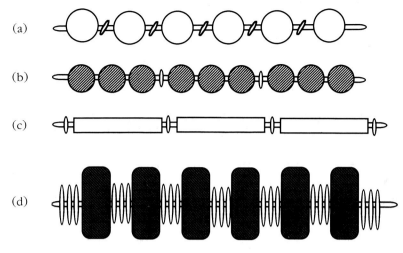

(a)

(b)

(c)

(d)

If the line to be followed is long, curved or meandering, it is probably better to fasten the thread holding the beads at the start of the line, but leave it free at the other end. Push the beads into place, stitching between them and over the thread, to the end of the line. Make sure, however, that the strung beads do not fall off the thread in the process. Use a very long thread or, better still, make a knot at the end.

Various decorative variations can be seen in the diagrams below, in which the thread is as much a part of the effect as the beads.

(Above)
(a) A string of beads couched to the fabric between every bead
(b) A string of beads couched between every third bead
(c) A string of bugles couched between every one
(d) A string of large beads couched with three stitches between each bead

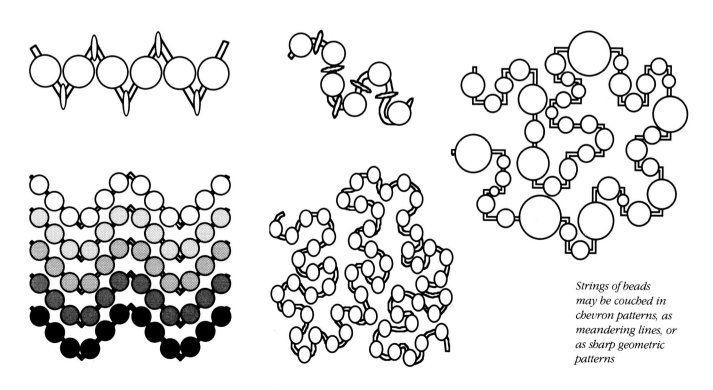

Strings of beads may be couched in chevron patterns, as meandering lines, or as sharp geometric patterns

(a) Lazy stitch may be worked either back and forth with a small stitch through the fabric at each end of the row; or

(b) as beaded satin stitch. The number of beads threaded may vary

(c) If the thread between every two or three beads is couched, then it is called spot or overlaid stitch

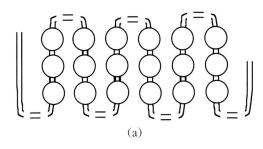

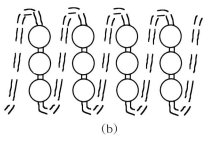

(a)

(b)

(Below)
Part of a Hungarian sleeve panel showing lazy stitch in bands between heavy stitchery

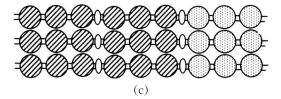

(c)

Lazy stitch

This gives an almost raised appearance to the beads. It is usually worked in bands, between two parallel lines, as solid beading.

Fasten the thread securely to the fabric and pick up a number of beads (usually between five and eight, but more if they are very small). Take the thread across and down into the fabric, checking that the length of the beads equals the length of the long stitch. Bring the thread up again, close to the point at which it went down. Pick up the same number of beads, going across to the other side. The fact that the thread is not couched down between the beads gives the raised effect.

Couching over a cord

A similar method is used to couch beads over a cord, giving a heavy, raised line. Select a thick, firm string or piping cord, and couch this in place on the fabric, following the line of the design. Whip or wrap the end of the cord to prevent it unravelling.

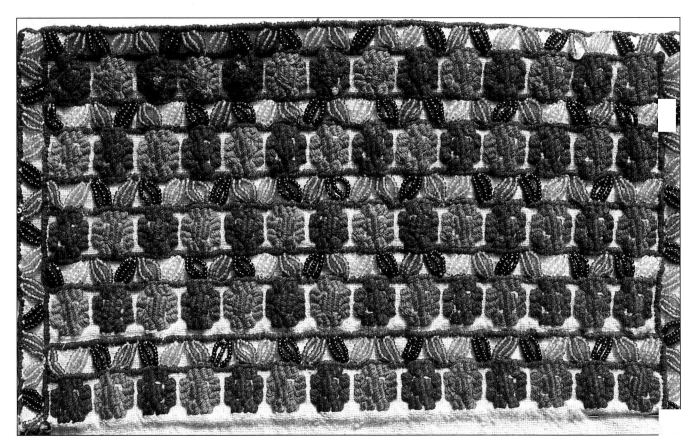

Thread a fine needle with strong cotton, bringing it up as close as possible to the side of the cord. Pick up as many beads as are required to go over the cord exactly, before taking the needle back into the fabric on the other side. Work as for satin stitch, coming up on the same side of the cord each time. This ensures that the rows of beads lie smoothly side by side, covering the cord completely.

When the design line has tight curves, less beads will be required on alternate rows around the curve to give a neat finish. If the cord itself is decorative, wrapped, dyed or space-dyed, the rows of beads can be spaced out to leave parts of the cord showing. Try criss-crossing lines of beads over the cord, or adding long straight stitches, thin ribbons or hand-embroidery stitches, in addition to the beads.

Couching over padding

Various methods for padded or raised areas of beads can be borrowed from other embroidery techniques, such as metal-thread work. Small areas of padded felt, built up in layers, can be covered with beads using lazy stitch (this would have to be used if the padding substance were too hard for the fine needles to penetrate). In all cases, the nature, size and height of the padding determines the method of covering with beads.

When the padding is decorative, such as gold, silver, copper or patterned leathers, parts of it may be left exposed. You could cover an area solidly with beads, which would act as the padding for more beads to be couched over them in parts.

MACHINE COUCHING

The preparation of stringing the beads is the same as for hand methods (see page 51). When using the machine to couch the beads down, however, the machine thread is nearly always more visible so bear this in mind when planning the colour scheme.

For machine couching you will need a swing-needle sewing machine that is capable of zigzag and satin stitch. The beads will obviously not pass under the normal presser foot, so remove this and lower the teeth or feed dog as for free machine

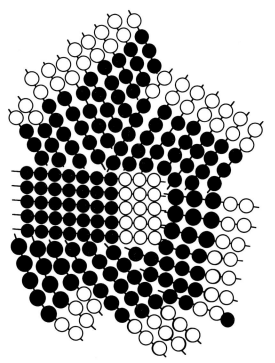

(Left)
Detail of part of a North American Indian nineteenth-century bag showing lazy stitch worked in different directions

(Below)
*Beads over a cord:
(a) the cord is sewn to a fabric and the ends secured with satin stitch
(b) an alternative method using machine zigzag
(c) the threaded beads are laid diagonally over the cord
(d) an alternative pattern*

(a)　　　　　(b)　　　　　(c)　　　　　(d)

embroidery. Your machine manual will tell you how to do this (often included under 'Darning'). Alternatively, use a special cording foot with a tunnel which allows the beads to pass through. Frame the fabric tightly in a ring frame, setting the machine to the maximum-width satin stitch. Do not forget to lower the presser-foot lever which engages the top tension system.

A panel showing couched beads over a fabric roll (Jan Hay)

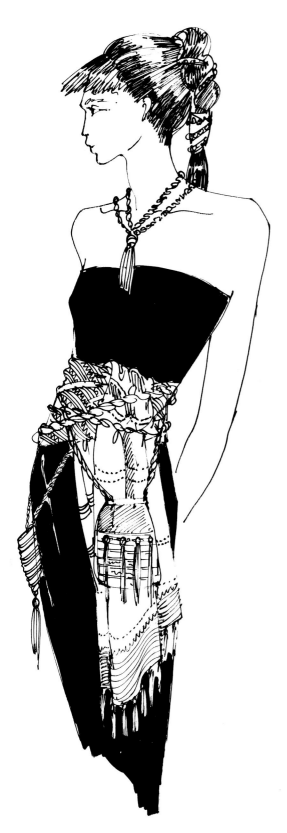

Begin by threading small beads on to a length of cotton, holding this firmly on the fabric behind and in front of the machine needle. The machine will stitch from side to side, over the threaded beads, with the stitches slipping between the beads. How quickly you stitch and move the frame will determine how much stitching is visible: there may be a bead between each zigzag, or virtually close satin stitch with the beads protruding through.

If you completely encase a bead with stitches, part the threads with a fingernail to expose the bead, or leave it hidden, as a mysterious bump in a row of satin stitch. A little practice will reveal so many possibilities, with variations in density of both the stitches and the beads.

When working in this way, people often worry that the machine needle will hit a bead. In reality, the beads seem to slip sideways but, if hit directly, it is more likely that the beads, rather than the needle, will break. To be on the safe side, however, use a stronger needle – perhaps size 100 or even 110 – and keep some spare needles in store.

A closer look at the panel, showing the couched metallic beads (Jan Hay)

(Left)
Suggestions for using couched beads among pleats, against embroidered stripes or over padding (Christina Barry).
See page 53 for more about beaded cords, as shown in the hair and around the neck

Bugles

Extra-long bugle beads can be very effectively couched by machine. It is an advantage to be able to cover part of their length with a dense area or 'blob' of satin stitch, with more open zigzag over the remainder of the bugle. This subdues the colour and shine of the bead and breaks up the visual impact of its length, integrating it beautifully with the surrounding fabric and stitching. Shaded, variegated and metallic machine-embroidery threads are particularly lovely when used in this way.

Larger beads

The size of bead which may be couched by machine is inevitably limited, both by the width of the sideways swing of the needle, and by the height to which the needle rises. Always err on the side of caution, as broken beads and needles are an unnecessary frustration.

A closer look at the couched beads (Christine Evans)

If you wish to couch large beads by machine – perhaps in a piece of machine embroidery – try the following method. Thread the beads on to a length of strong cotton. Frame the fabric as before, remove the presser foot and lower the teeth or feed dog. Set the machine for free running stitch. Stitch at right angles to the line of threaded beads, making short rows of stitching, to and fro, between the beads, to secure them to the fabric.

Fringing effects

Using free running stitch, machine over the thread holding the beads to anchor them firmly to the fabric. Hold a length or loop of the beaded thread to one side before stitching to secure it again to the fabric. This will give regular or random-length loops of beads hanging freely from the surface or edge of the fabric. These loops may be completely covered with beads, or worked so that part of the thread is seen with clusters of beads which will fall to the ends of the loops.

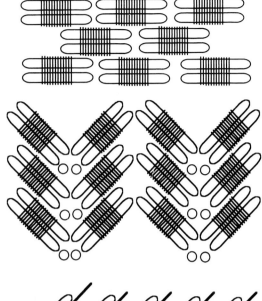

Strings of bugles may be couched with satin stitch, either by hand or machine, and round beads or couched threads added

(Below)
Round beads and discs sewn to a metallic fabric, and strung to give a more solid band
(Jill Izzard)

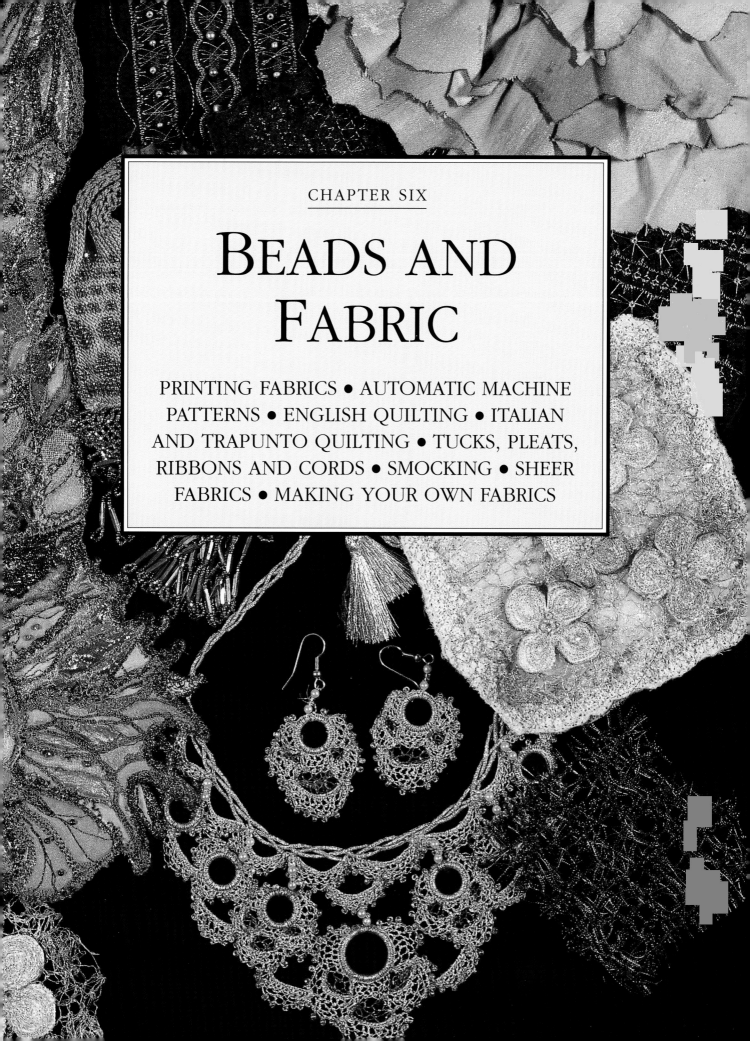

CHAPTER SIX

BEADS AND FABRIC

PRINTING FABRICS • AUTOMATIC MACHINE
PATTERNS • ENGLISH QUILTING • ITALIAN
AND TRAPUNTO QUILTING • TUCKS, PLEATS,
RIBBONS AND CORDS • SMOCKING • SHEER
FABRICS • MAKING YOUR OWN FABRICS

(Below) *Exploring the theme of icons, using hand-made felt, painted fabrics, beads, bells and metallic beads* (Jill Izzard)

Beads alter the very nature of fabric, perhaps more than any other embroidery technique or stitch. Apart from the actual sight of the beads, they provide a surface texture and a tactile quality, as well as adding weight, which changes the way the fabric handles and drapes. Beads become the focal point in a design, adding glimmer and shine. It follows, therefore, that the beads and fabric to be used together should be chosen with great care. The golden rules are to avoid dotting beads around indiscriminately in the hope of adding zest to a piece of work or, worse, to add them as an afterthought.

Some fabrics have a surface texture which lends itself to the addition of beads. They nestle into the pile of velvet and the channels of corduroy, and sink into the rough surface of handmade felt. Try pressing small beads – either singly or strung on to threads – into handmade paper while it is still damp. Smooth fabrics may be tucked, pleated, quilted, smocked, densely machine-stitched, torn into strips or textured with stitch patterns, giving that exciting combination of beads and fabric which complement each other perfectly.

PRINTING FABRICS

Dyeing, space-dyeing, marbling, painting, printing or transfer-printing your own fabrics is always an excellent starting point for embroidery. The shapes, colours and patterns of beads can play an actual, as well as inspirational, part in these processes. Perhaps it is the metallic, multi-coloured glow of beads which suggests the colours to be used on the fabric.

Printing patterns can reflect the circles and lines of different-sized beads, sequins and bugles. These shapes are found in the poker-pen attachments which may be used to burn or singe patterns on to fabrics, and look unbelievably like beads and sequins. Marbling with gold or silver oil or enamel paints gives swirling patterns and shapes, just waiting to be enhanced with little metallic beads.

Whatever your favourite method of colouring fabric is, do consider fabric, threads and beads together.

(Pages 58 and 59)
*Wire and wood
frames, wrapped with
strung beads and
stitched to make a
fabric, samples of this
wire-frame fabric,
samples of quilting
with beads, machine-
stitched flowers with
beaded centres, a
Victorian miser purse,
a painted felt sample
(Joan Bowen), a
quilted and beaded
collar* (Sue Fenwick),
*a necklace and
earrings in machine-
made lace with beads
(Delia Pusey) and
a sample showing
painted, smocked
and beaded fabric*
(Diana Morgans)

*Beads and sequins
on painted felt, on a
background of painted
papers* (Jill Izzard)

*Detail of massed beads
on painted felt, with
machine embroidery
backed with painted
papers* (Jill Izzard)

(Opposite)
*Three samples of
machine stitching, with
automatic patterns on
the front and back of
velvet and organza
with added tassels*

AUTOMATIC MACHINE PATTERNS

Modern electric sewing machines have a range of utility and decorative patterns which may not appear, at first glance, to have any affinity with beadwork. They can, however, serve a very useful purpose.

Lines of automatic patterns strengthen and stabilize a fabric, giving body to support the weight of beads. The majority of patterns also have a structure or grid. Regard this as a way of getting the design on to the fabric, with the grid indicating the possible placement of the beads. Even the simplest line of open zigzag could have a small bead sewn by hand on the point of each 'V'. Try threading narrow ribbon through a stitched pattern, securing this in place with the addition of beads placed along the line.

As always with automatic patterns, the best effects are achieved by building up layers of a pattern – stitching massed lines together or over each other – rather than a single line. Add to this texture with beads and handstitchery, perhaps using a composite stitch such as raised-chain band or Pekinese stitch.

Automatic patterns worked on velvet appear quite subtle, with the stitches sinking into the pile of the fabric. Try working on the wrong side of the fabric too, so that the reverse of the stitch is seen on the right side. This is often far more interesting than the intended pattern.

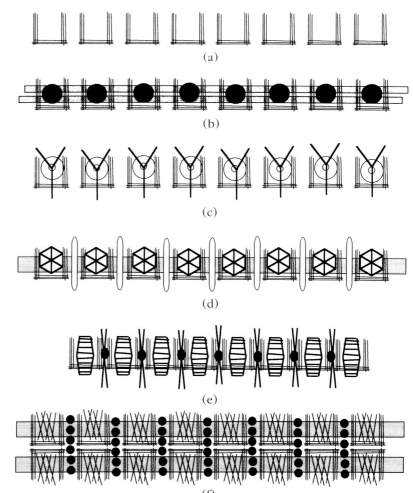

(a)

(b)

(c)

(d)

(e)

(f)

(Above)
Beads with automatic patterns:
(a) a simple machine-stitched pattern
(b) ribbon is threaded through and a bead sewn within each section
(c) a sequin may be stitched on using fly stitch
(d) jewels and bugles give a richer effect
(e) home-made beads and small glass beads held with long stitches
(f) two lines of pattern threaded with ribbons, couched beads or lazy stitch and herringbone stitches

Suggestions for a jacket or a waistcoat using the velvet and organza samples on the previous page
(Christina Barry)

padded areas of fabric. This contrast of shadows may be emphasized further with beads, densely packed into the stitched areas or along the lines. An all-over quilted pattern of meandering vermicelli stitch, worked as free machine embroidery, provides an exciting foil and base for beads.

Beads add an extra dimension to a quilted geometric or grid pattern. They can be massed into certain parts of the grid, along the lines, at the intersections or grouped in corners of the squares. Cut shapes of handmade, dyed felt, built up in overlapping layers, give a wonderfully rich texture. Machine stitching and beads sink into the surface, providing a contrast to the surface of the felt.

ITALIAN AND TRAPUNTO QUILTING

Both of these quilting techniques are stitched through two fabrics – a top and a backing – with the padded areas added afterwards. In Italian quilting, the pattern is usually based on curved parallel lines of stitching, with quilting or thick wool threaded through the channels. In trapunto quilting, small shapes are stitched around, before being padded from behind. The backing fabric is carefully slit within the shape to allow wadding to be pushed in, giving a raised effect on the front of the work. A Victorian technique of working lazy stitch over trapunto shapes adds tone to beads and sequins and gives a rich, undulating effect. Pull the thread tight in every row to keep the beads secure.

In shadow trapunto quilting, the top layer of fabric is sheer and translucent. This allows the colour of the padding to show through on the front of the work. Try mixing scraps of thread, coloured fleece and little beads for the padding, to give extra interest to the raised shapes. The lines and shapes of these forms of quilting may be emphasized by adding clusters of beads, packed closely to the raised, smooth areas of fabric.

ENGLISH QUILTING

English quilting is a technique admirably suited to the addition of beads. The sandwich of three layers, consisting of the top fabric, the wadding (batting) and the backing fabric, supports the weight of the beads.

The beauty of quilting lies in the contrast between the dense, stitched areas and the plain,

TUCKS, PLEATS, RIBBONS AND CORDS

These techniques provide ways of adding texture to a background fabric. Tucks and pleats are stitched into the fabric, ribbons and cords are

Collar combining quilting with cutwork in a variety of fabrics, machine embroidery and beads (Sue Fenwick)

applied to it, with the possibility of combining any or all of them together. Whichever techniques you choose, they will suggest where to add the beads for maximum effect.

Close lines of pin tucks, spaced regularly or at random on a fine silk fabric, would be greatly enhanced by adding rows of little beads or pearls between them. Imagine this in shades of cream, or perhaps black, for a simple but stunning evening waistcoat. Try working lines or a grid pattern of pin tucks on the machine, with a bead sewn into the pin tucks at intervals to flatten them.

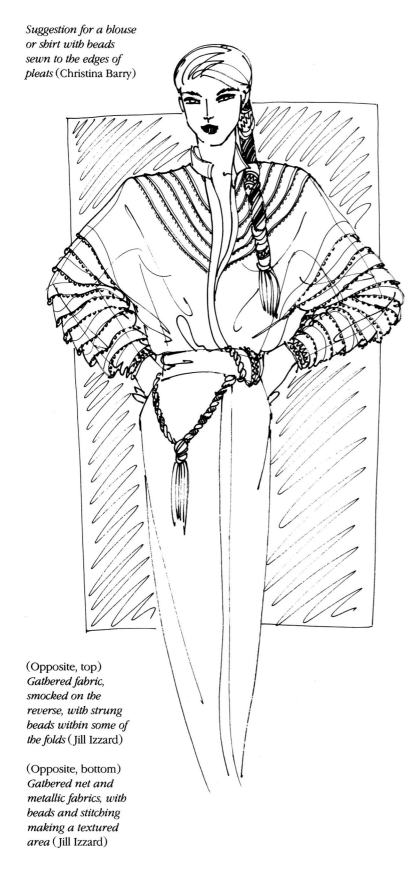

Suggestion for a blouse or shirt with beads sewn to the edges of pleats (Christina Barry)

(Opposite, top) *Gathered fabric, smocked on the reverse, with strung beads within some of the folds* (Jill Izzard)

(Opposite, bottom) *Gathered net and metallic fabrics, with beads and stitching making a textured area* (Jill Izzard)

Sew beads to the edges of overlapping pleats, worked horizontally. The added weight would make the pleats hang well, but imagine, too, what would happen if the pleats were worked vertically. The beads would distort the way the folded edge behaved and, on the right fabric, could look equally attractive. Hanging strands of beads – a type of fringe – may be inserted beneath narrow pleats, either worked regularly or in groups.

The range of ribbons available has increased greatly in recent years. Beads sewn on to patterned ribbons, either within their width or on the edges, add to their rich, decorative quality. Massed lines of machine stitching or automatic patterns add weight and strength to ribbons, seeming to enhance the way they curl and twist. Experiment with massed rows of beaded ribbons, side by side, or curl, twist, pleat and gather them before applying to a background fabric. Any remaining visible fabric would, of course, be densely stitched with more beads.

The method of creating machine-wrapped cords is described on page 116. Like ribbons, all cords, whether bought, handmade or machine-wrapped, may be twisted, looped or knotted and sewn on to a background fabric either in traditional or very free patterns. Beads may be added to the cords, by hand or by machine, or to the fabric in the shapes and alongside the lines created by the cords. Again, the raised pattern makes the beads an integral and necessary part of the design.

SMOCKING

Smocking is a traditional and familiar way of manipulating a fabric surface, and specialist books are available on the techniques involved. Here are some suggestions on how to incorporate beads into smocking in new and exciting ways for both practical and experimental purposes.

Work lines of gathering across the area to be smocked, and pull these up to form pleats or reeds. Hold these reeds in place with patterns of stitching before removing the gathering threads. Many of the smocking stitch patterns can have some or all of the holding stitches replaced with beads.

This technique is particularly effective with honeycomb smocking. The beads may be added during the actual stitching process of holding the reeds together, or the reeds may be worked using a thicker decorative thread with the beads added later. Alternatively, the hollows formed by honeycomb smocking may be filled with massed little beads, leaving the ridges of fabric to form a grid pattern of contrast.

Reverse smocking is prepared in the same way, with gathering threads used to pull the fabric into reeds. Cable stitch is worked across the back of the work to hold the reeds in place. This offers enormous scope on the front for free, experimental work, distorting and twisting the reeds before adding beads and stitchery. Sew beads individually, pushing them between the reeds so that they are half-hidden by the folds of fabric. Use lengths of strung beads couched between the reeds, densely in parts and sparsely in others, or hanging freely.

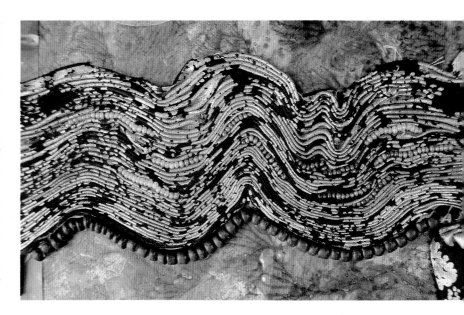

SHEER FABRICS

The manipulation of sheer fabrics into soft, ruched textures gives yet more scope for clusters of beads. Perhaps the attraction is the ultimate contrast between the delicacy of the fabric, seeming to enfold the hardness of the bead.

Organza is available in many colours, as well as in shot and metallic combinations. As with all sheer fabrics, layers, fragments and strips give even more tonal variations, mirroring the reflective qualities of the beads themselves. Organdie, muslins, bandage strips and nets are often better torn than cut with scissors. Depending on the nature of the design, the sheer fabrics may be

(Below)
Scrim, knitting ribbon, machine embroidery and beads give a rich texture (Elsie Probert)

(Bottom)
Beads sewn to painted scrim, which has been ruched and applied to painted bubble plastic (Jill Izzard)

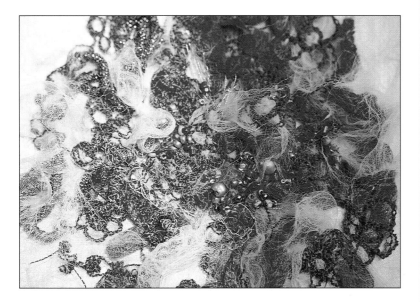

bonded to a base fabric with Vilene Bondaweb, or applied more freely with hand or machine stitching.

Contrast transparent, opaque and pearly beads to create different effects in the design. The transparent beads will reflect the colour of beads next to them and the colour of the thread running through them, as well as the layers of fabric beneath.

MAKING YOUR OWN FABRICS

Most embroiderers are fascinated by the techniques which enable them to create the whole fabric, as opposed to merely embellishing a purchased material. The various ways of making a fabric all offer endless possibilities for incorporating beads, adding richness, texture and a gloriously tactile surface quality.

(Opposite page, right) Panel using transparent fabrics, machine embroidery, beads and sequins (Sue Aubertin). A detail of the panel is shown overleaf (top)

Designs based on Indian patterns and experimental samples of techniques (Sue Aubertin)

Wire frames

You will not need to purchase expensive equipment as simple, home-made frames are quite adequate. The main requirements are that the frame is rigid, and thin enough to pass under the needle of your sewing machine. Strong wire or a metal coathanger may be cut and bent into a square or rectangular shape with the two ends either soldered or bound together with sticky tape. Alternatively, you could buy a filet-lace frame from a specialist supplier. Although a temporary frame can be cut from strong card, a wire frame will be more durable.

The basic technique is to wrap threads and beads round the frame, in either one or both directions, and to secure these with stitching to form a fabric, which is then cut from the frame. You have total control over how firm or lacy you wish the fabric to be, depending on the weight of the threads used, how closely they are wrapped and how much stitching and beading is added.

(Above)
Detail of the panel on page 68, showing massed beads stitched in cross shapes and triangles
(Sue Aubertin)

(Right)
Computer Cat, *a panel combining painted fabrics and machine embroidery with beaded wire-frame fabric. This panel was designed on a computer*
(Margaret Charlton)

(Far right)
Detail of the wire-frame beaded fabric applied to a machine-embroidered triangle
(Margaret Charlton)

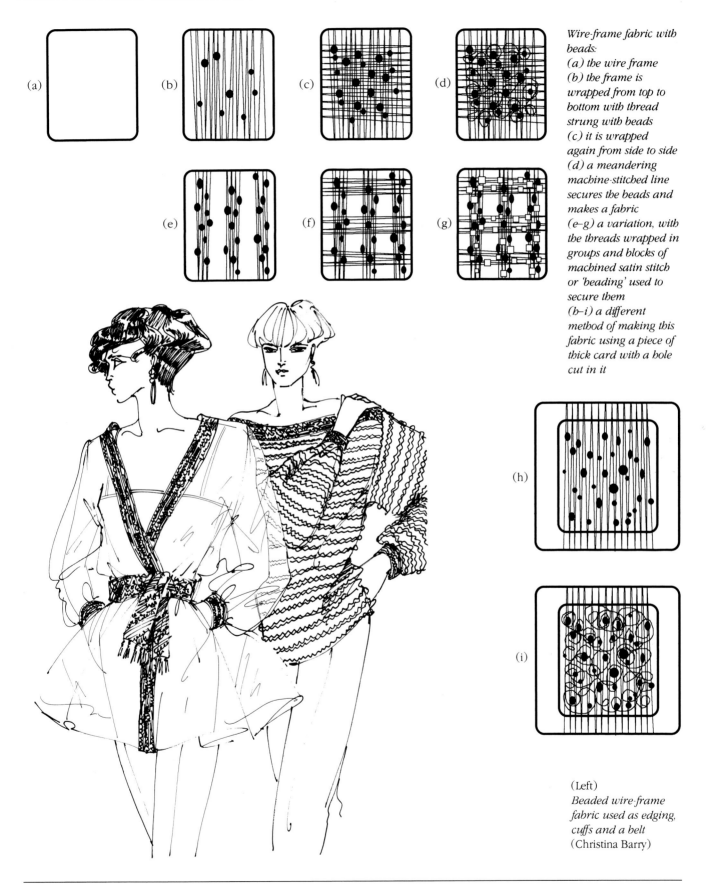

Wire-frame fabric with
beads:
(a) the wire frame
(b) the frame is
wrapped from top to
bottom with thread
strung with beads
(c) it is wrapped
again from side to side
(d) a meandering
machine-stitched line
secures the beads and
makes a fabric
(e–g) a variation, with
the threads wrapped in
groups and blocks of
machined satin stitch
or 'beading' used to
secure them
(h–i) a different
method of making this
fabric using a piece of
thick card with a hole
cut in it

(Left)
Beaded wire-frame
fabric used as edging,
cuffs and a belt
(Christina Barry)

Choose a range of threads: thick, thin, smooth and textured. Tie one end on to the frame, wrapping it round and round or in a figure-of-eight pattern. Decide how closely you want to wrap and whether to add threads in the other direction too. Tie off the end of the thread to the frame. Thread your beads on to a long length of strong cotton and wrap round the frame on top of the already wrapped threads. You can push the beads along the threads, repositioning them as required, while adding the stitching.

Use a toning or metallic thread on your machine, remove the presser foot and lower the feed dog or teeth. This will enable you to stitch freely in any direction. Even though your manual may advise the use of a darning foot for free embroidery, this is not possible with this technique, as the foot will catch on both the threads and the beads. Stitch close, parallel lines or a meandering, all-over pattern. With practice, the needle will seem to slip easily between the beads even when they are threaded closely together, but, as a precaution, run the machine a little more slowly than usual. The resulting fabric is remarkably strong and handles beautifully.

Slits may be incorporated by stitching a little way across the threads and then back again, repeating this on the other side of the frame. String beads across or down the slits, continuing them on to the fabric itself.

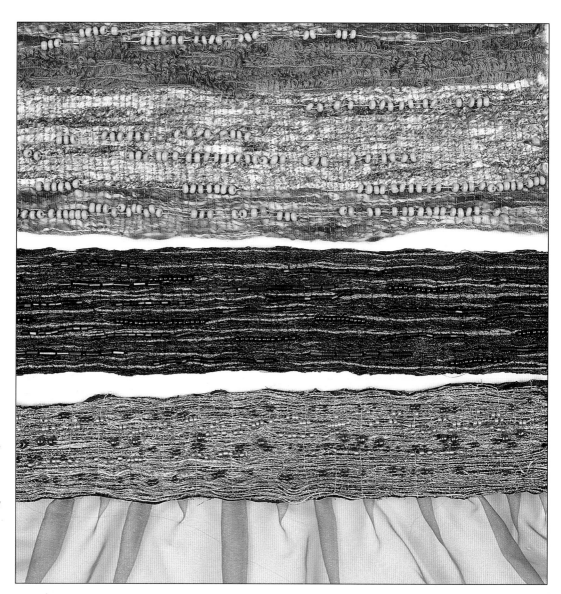

Cuffs made of beaded wire-frame fabric. One is of metallic threads and beads, sewn to an organza sleeve; another is similar; and the pink one combines slub knitting yarns and matt-pink beads intended for use with a knitted jacket

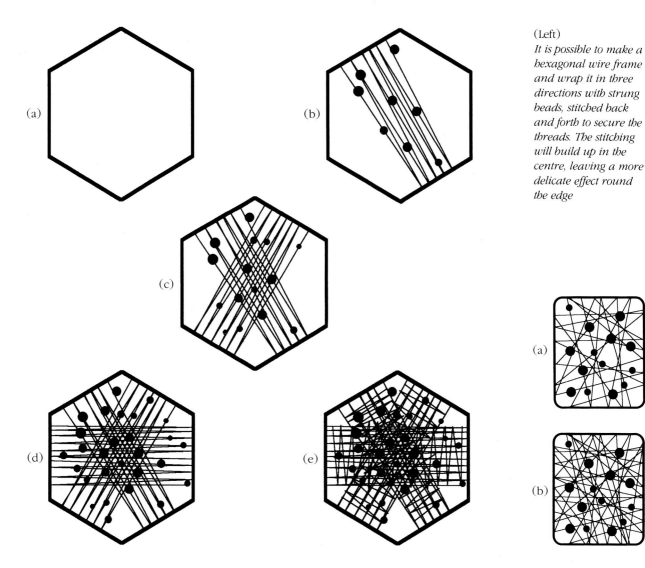

It is possible to make a hexagonal wire frame and wrap it in three directions with strung beads, stitched back and forth to secure the threads. The stitching will build up in the centre, leaving a more delicate effect round the edge

(Above)
A more random method of wrapping the wire frame with strung beads

The diagrams and illustrations in this chapter show a variety of interpretations on this theme. A delicate, lacy effect may be achieved by threading beads on to a fine machine-embroidery thread, which is then used to wrap the frame freely in both directions. As you wrap, position the beads singly or in groups. Add free machine stitching to form a mesh-like beaded web.

Water-soluble fabric

Two water-soluble fabrics are now available, one of which works in hot or boiling water and the other in cold water. Work free machine stitching in a connected pattern of circles or meandering lines. When the work is immersed in water, the fabric dissolves, leaving only the stitching. A further dimension may be given to this technique by adding beads which are suspended in the lacy web of threads. Work the basic pattern of stitched circles and lines on the framed fabric. Thread small beads on to a long piece of toning cotton. Attach the end of this thread to part of the machined pattern with a few stitches on the spot. Work free machining, going over parts of the pattern and the beading thread, releasing beads as you go. The point of a needle or a stiletto is useful to position the beads while you stitch.

Although it is only possible to make relatively small pieces of 'fabric' by these methods, they can be used in so many ways. Join pieces to make garments such as waistcoats, use them for cuffs on jackets or knitwear, for jewellery and accessories, or use strips as insertions between ribbons or other fabrics. Imagine a precious little bag made of your own bead-encrusted fabric.

Two papier-maché bowls, pleated fabrics, machine-made lace using water-soluble fabric, and painted pearls and beads
(Delia Pusey)

Solid machine stitching

This is yet another way of making a fabric, and is very suitable for small, undulating shapes. Bond felt and calico together with Vilene Bondaweb, to produce a firm fabric to support the dense free-machine running stitch and, of course, the beads. Mark round each required shape using a template. Cut out the shapes.

You will find it very much easier to machine on these small pieces if they are first supported on an old pair of tights. Using an embroidery ring frame, push the complete circle of the frame down the leg section (with a wooden ring frame, this is the inner circle, and with a metal spring frame, it is the outer circle). Stretch the tights as firmly as you can in the frame, before cutting away the excess tights from around the edge. You will now be machining on a single layer of the tights. Place the felt and calico shapes on to the tights, calico-side uppermost. Set your machine for free running stitch, removing the presser foot and replacing it with a darning foot if you wish. Lower the teeth or feed dog, remembering to lower the presser-foot lever to engage the top-tension system of the machine. Work massed lines of running stitch round the shape, continuing until none of the calico remains visible. The more you stitch, the more the shape will curl and undulate.

When the stitching is complete, remove the frame from the machine and, while still held taut in the frame, cut away the tights from around the stitched shape. Squares, circles or flower and leaf shapes may be overlapped, the pieces pulled and distorted to form bowl-like creations which are ideal receptacles for beads. The richness of this technique, especially when worked with the darker metallic threads, combines beautifully with dense areas of beads or bead weaving.

Machine-stitched Tudor roses with beaded centres and machine-wrapped beaded cords

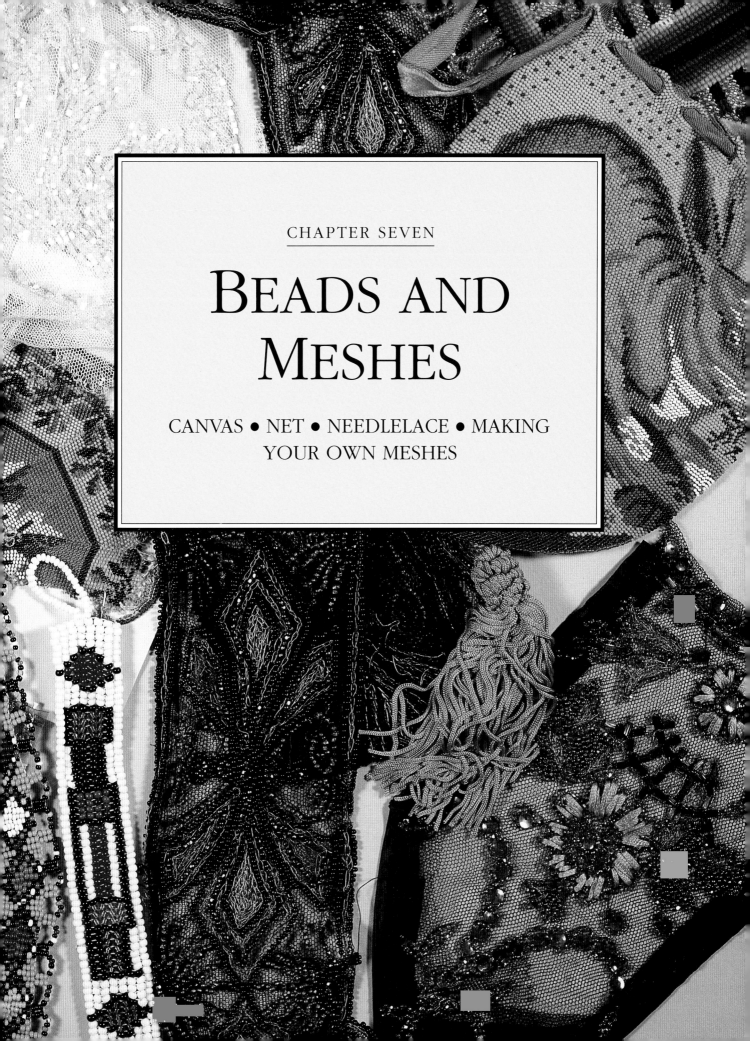

CHAPTER SEVEN

BEADS AND MESHES

CANVAS • NET • NEEDLELACE • MAKING
YOUR OWN MESHES

(Previous page)
*Four Victorian canvas
bags* (one by
permission of Sheila
Paine), *Zulu
beadwork bracelets,
four samples of 1920s
beading on net,
samples of beading
on rug canvas and
beaded meshes worked
on a wire frame*

Meshed fabrics are ideal for embroidering and embellishing with beads. Beads can be used on a variety of bought and home-made meshes.

CANVAS

Although canvas is an open-weave mesh, it is strong and durable, and therefore ideal to use as a base for beadwork. This was much exploited by the Victorians, who developed a particular style of work during the mid-nineteenth century. Berlin woolwork charts became available in this country

in about 1830, and, by the middle of the century, special beads from France and Germany were being imported for use with these charts.

Each bead took the place of a single tent stitch. The designs were mostly floral, with every imaginable article being worked, either entirely in beads or with the design itself in beads and the background in tent stitch using wool. Tea cosies, firescreens, mantel covers, footstools, bags, slippers, bellpulls and cushions were among the most popular items. A particular craze developed for grisaille beadwork, which used monochromatic beads – both clear and opaque – in black, grey and white, often combined with steel beads.

Day Aurora with the
Genius of Light, *a
beadwork picture or
firescreen panel
worked in about 1860.
The double canvas is
sewn with grey, white
and clear glass beads
in the style of grisaille
beadwork* (From the
Embroiderers' Guild
collection)

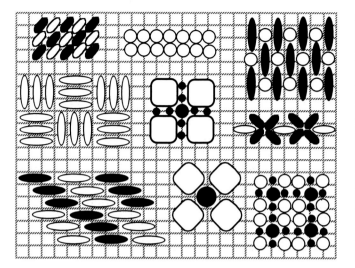

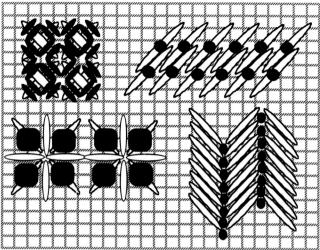

(Above left)
Beads sewn on to canvas, either over an intersection, or over two or three threads of canvas in a straight line

(Above right)
Beads replacing some of the stitches in conventional canvaswork

Victorian bags embroidered in a variety of techniques popular at the time. (Top right) Bag in linen canvas embroidered in silk and wool with faceted steel beads (Bottom left) Canvaswork bag (Bottom right) Beaded bag imitating North American Indian techniques (From the Embroiderers' Guild collection)

Florentine stitching on canvas with an added 'tassel' of lustre beads, tiny metallic beads and sequins

(Below)
A freer approach to beaded canvas:
(a) small pieces of distorted canvas laid on top of each other on a background fabric and invisibly stitched down
(b) sequins, bugles and beads make a rich, shiny texture over an area

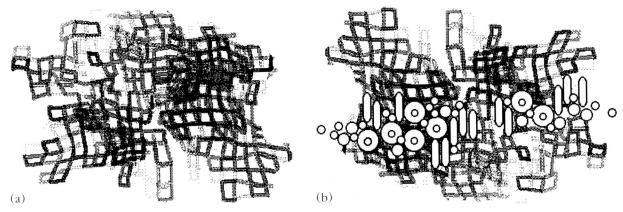

(a)   (b)

The use of beads on canvas continued to be a popular technique well into the twentieth century. Variations developed, such as stitching monochromatic beads and sequins on black fabric or net. More of the canvas was worked with stitches (including straight stitches), with beads and bugles added in parts of the design.

In today's canvaswork a much freer approach may be taken, while still making use of the strength of the mesh to support the weight of the beads. Areas of the canvas can be painted and left unworked, holes cut with beads threaded across the open spaces, and machine zigzag and satin stitch worked over parts of the mesh. Try working little squares of richly encrusted beads and stitches, and cut them out, overlap them slightly, or position them irregularly, before machining them on to another fabric.

Canvas is often thought of as a very flat medium, but this does not have to be the case. Work areas of stitches on canvas, leaving gaps between them. Dampen the canvas, squeezing it tightly in your hand to crease and distort it. Leave it like this, crunched up, to dry overnight. You can then apply it to another piece of canvas or fabric, exploiting the humps, bumps and distortions. Fill the areas left unstitched with beads, which will act as the means of securing one to the other. Experimental perhaps, but a fun way of achieving a very rich and textured surface.

(a)

(b)

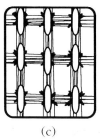

(c)

(Above)
Mesh using the wire-frame method:
(a) the thread is used to wrap the frame in groups in both directions
(b) it is secured with satin-stitch blobs
(c) oval beads are sewn on by hand

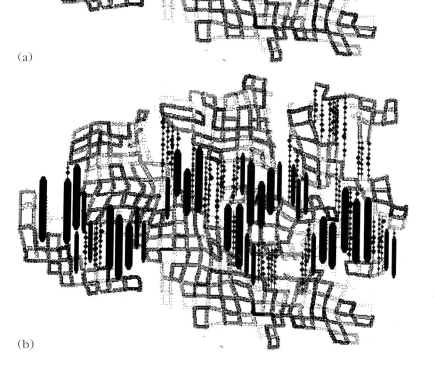

(a)

(b)

(Above left and left)
A variation on the example opposite, also using distorted pieces of mesh fabrics (a), decorated with bugles and strings of couched beads (b)

Dress net with beads held within the hexagonal holes

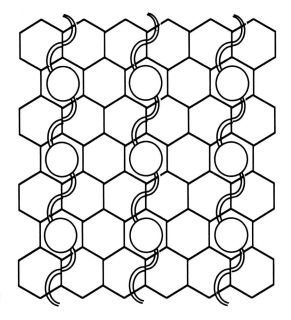

NET

Although net may appear flimsy, it is strong enough to support small beads and sequins. The added weight makes the net handle and drape beautifully. Net embroidery with beads was another Victorian passion, with the beads held within the hexagonal holes, rather than on top of the net. Traditionally, this is a counted-thread or darning technique, with shapes worked in a variety of filling stitches and with small beads. Floral and geometric patterns were the favourite designs. Although historical pieces are wonderful, treasured examples of technique, it is exciting to try something new, and to add texture and richness to the surface.

Using a strong net, work random lines of darning using space-dyed, metallic or textured threads, thin ribbons or ribbon yarn. Add masses of little beads in areas, pile them up or let them hang freely as strands. Nylon net comes in rather harsh colours and will not readily take dyes or fabric paint. Silk net, however, available from the bridal departments of large stores, may be dyed or space-dyed in soft, subtle colours. Experiment with ruching or gathering the net, tearing it into strips, and applying it to a background fabric. Fill in the resulting folds and hollows with beads and pearls of different sizes.

Lacis or filet darning is a simple lace form consisting of patterns woven or darned into square-mesh knotted net. This was rarely worked with beads, but square-mesh net is a very versatile medium in either fine or coarse weights, regular or irregular weave or handmade. Suspend beads and bugles within the square holes, over the intersections or along the warp and weft threads. Darn ribbons, strips of torn net or fabric and cords through the mesh, adding beads to hold them in place. Whatever net you have, try pulling it in different directions to distort it. This will need to be sewn to a backing fabric to hold the distortions in place, but often this gives more exciting results than the purely geometric grid pattern.

Layers of net laid on a fabric backing and secured with running stitches and stitched beads

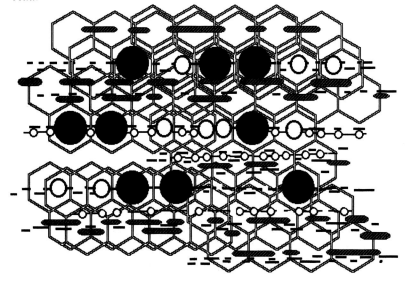

NEEDLELACE

For some people, the mention of lace brings to mind bobbins and fine white edgings. Needlelace, as the name implies, is worked with a needle and

Dress net zigzagged by machine to give extra colour and texture. Free running stitch is worked across the spaces and beads are added by hand, darning and stitching into the net and machine stitching

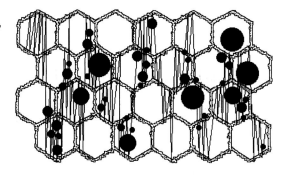

thread, and very exciting, modern, colourful and textured lace is now being produced. Beads may be sewn in as the work progresses, or stitched on to a piece of completed lace. The basic stitch of needlelace is a detached buttonhole or Brussels stitch. Any good book on needlelace will give many more stitches and the methods needed to make them.

A hat made with a variety of needlelace techniques, with beads sewn on to emphasize the colour and texture (Ros Hills)

Experiment by framing a piece of fabric and working a line of small running stitches. Using a fairly fine needle and thread, make a detached buttonhole stitch into the first running stitch. Pick up a small bead, make another buttonhole stitch, then add a bead, continuing in this way across the row and subsequent rows. The working thread only goes into the fabric at each side. Keeping the tension correct is obviously a big part of the experienced laceworker's skill. The aim here is to enjoy adding beads to the framework of detached stitches, making, perhaps, just a little pocket or flap to begin with. At intervals, you could add two or three beads, big or small beads, or alter the tension on purpose. The results may be surprisingly exciting. Those with more experience of needlelace will enjoy adding beads to this beautiful technique.

*A bag made using
similar needlelace
techniques, with beads
added to one area at
the base* (Ros Hills)

MAKING YOUR OWN MESHES

Zigzagged net threaded with textured yarns, laid on a fabric and beads stitched on

Use a wire frame as described on pages 70–3. Tie the end of a ball of thin string to one side of the frame (you could use a cotton thread or double knitting wool for a softer mesh if you prefer). Wrap round and round the frame, horizontally and vertically, in either a regular or irregular pattern.

Thread your sewing machine, lower the feed dog or teeth and remove the presser foot (you may wish to replace this with a darning foot if you have one). Set your machine for a medium-width satin stitch, remembering to lower the presser-foot lever to engage the top-tension system. Zigzag over the string in both directions, interlocking the lines together to make a mesh fabric. Stitching over a second time will give a firmer finish. It is surprising just how strong the mesh becomes. This may consist of a very open pattern or lines close together, depending on how you wrapped the frame in the first place.

When the stitching is complete, cut the mesh from the frame, letting the loose ends of the string form part of the overall effect. Add beads by hand, spacing them regularly in the holes, in random clusters, on the intersections or threaded through the mesh.

Do not worry if your mesh grid is a little haphazard, as this is often the most attractive part of the effect. Try using metal threads for the machine stitching, and then placing it on a dark velvet background fabric. Add lots of little metallic beads in the holes, sewn on by hand – a simple but very effective idea for areas on fashion garments or an evening bag. Small pieces of mesh may be joined together to make larger items, but remember that layers or overlapping pieces always look more exciting than a single layer.

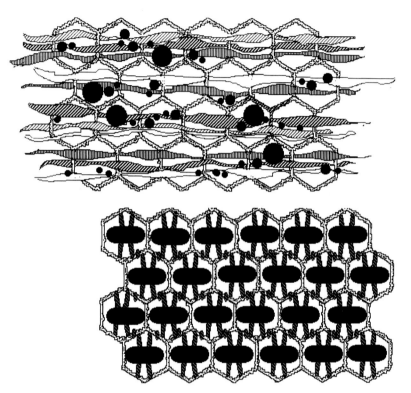

(Above)
Zigzagged net hand-wrapped with thread, which also holds the beads in the spaces. These flat beads have sideways holes through the narrowest part

Pulled work using a machine zigzag on scrim, with beads added to the spaces (Sarah Wiggs)

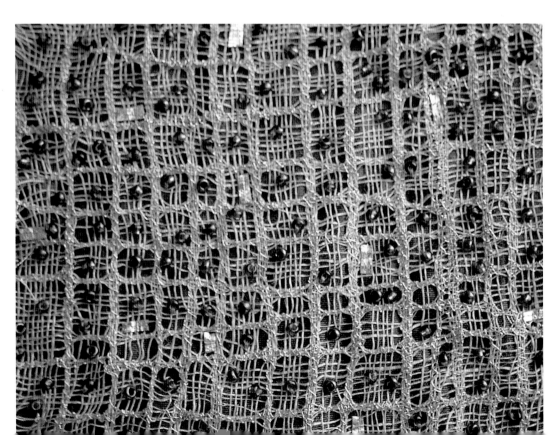

Mesh on water-soluble fabric

A softer and more regular mesh may be made on water-soluble fabric, as described on page 73. Draw a grid with a soft pencil and ruler on either hot- or cold-water-soluble fabric. The lines can be quite close together, spaced further apart or at random. Add diagonal lines as well, if you wish.

Frame the water-soluble fabric in a ring frame and prepare your machine for free stitching. Work a combination of lines of free running stitch and zigzag over the pencil-drawn grid in all directions. Remember to 'lock' the stitching together, going over each line several times, or the mesh will fall apart when the fabric is dissolved. You could lay a length of perle cotton or soft embroidery cotton along the lines prior to stitching, which will give a heavier mesh, as well as ensuring that the whole is locked together.

When the stitching is complete, remove from the frame, cutting away the excess fabric close to the stitched lines. Place into gently boiling or cold water, depending on the type of fabric you have used. The mesh will crinkle up alarmingly at this stage, but it can be pinned out to shape on a foam block or tile and left to dry. Sew on beads of various sizes and textures, bugles or sequins by hand to decorate the mesh.

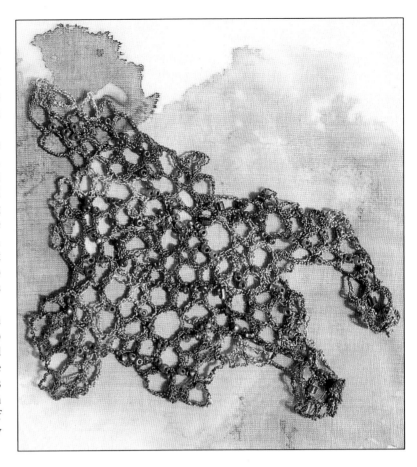

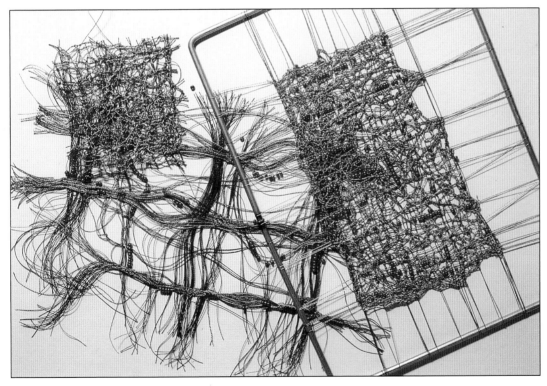

(Above)
A new fabric made by stitching on water-soluble fabric and then sewing the beads on to it

Mesh made by wrapping a wire frame with threaded beads, with stitching to secure them

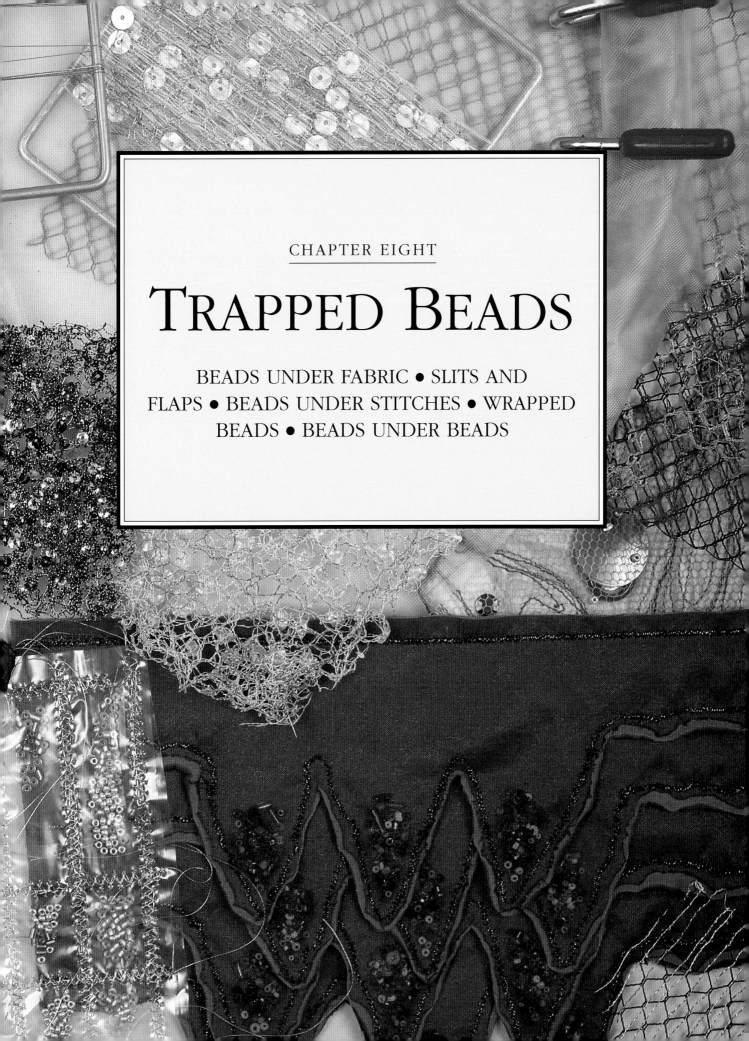

CHAPTER EIGHT

TRAPPED BEADS

BEADS UNDER FABRIC • SLITS AND
FLAPS • BEADS UNDER STITCHES • WRAPPED
BEADS • BEADS UNDER BEADS

(Below)
(a) Large sequins trapped under a sheer fabric, which is slit to reveal some of the shine and colour. Large and small cross stitches secure the fabric and more sequins to a backing (b) A variation which includes sequins and small pieces of fabric trapped between the slit fabric and a backing fabric. Running stitches secure the sequins and the slits are emphasized with massed small beads sewn on

There is something definitely mysterious about trapped beads, in the way that they are precious, hidden away, half-glimpsed through sheer fabric or partly wrapped with threads. Many of the suggestions in this chapter are based on very practical methods of attaching beads, jewels, sequins and *shisha*, but with new and decorative twists.

BEADS UNDER FABRIC

Placing sheer fabrics or net over beads serves several purposes, one of which is to subdue the harsh or too brightly-coloured beads that we all seem to possess. But, more than that, interesting colour changes take place when, for example, red beads are placed under a blue organza, so that they appear to be all shades of purple. Beads in the primary colours, placed under black organza, change to rich jewel colours which can be used to create wonderful effects.

Adapt the technique of shadow trapunto quilting (see page 64) by stitching raised clusters of beads to a background fabric before covering the area with a translucent fabric. Stitch round the beaded shapes, possibly with added beads, before slashing the top sheer fabric to expose the beads underneath. This could be done with a poker pen, adding an irregular, burnt edge, for added interest.

Consider whether it is always necessary to sew the beads to the background fabric. Perhaps they could move freely within the stitched shape of the sheer fabric, adding changing patterns to the embroidery. In this case, it would obviously not be a good idea to slash the top fabric.

A natural progression from placing beads under fabric would be to make small stitched pockets to hold the beads, attaching these to the background fabric along the top edge only. You could use different-sized and different-shaped pockets; overlapped, needlelace pockets; beads sewn to the edges of the pockets as well as beads contained within – the possibilities are endless.

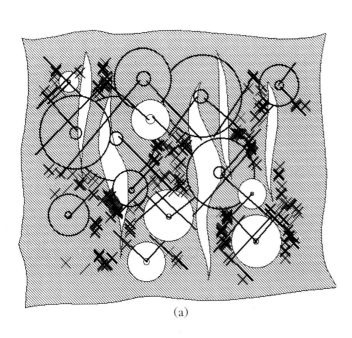

(a)

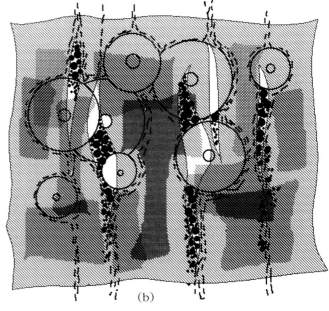

(b)

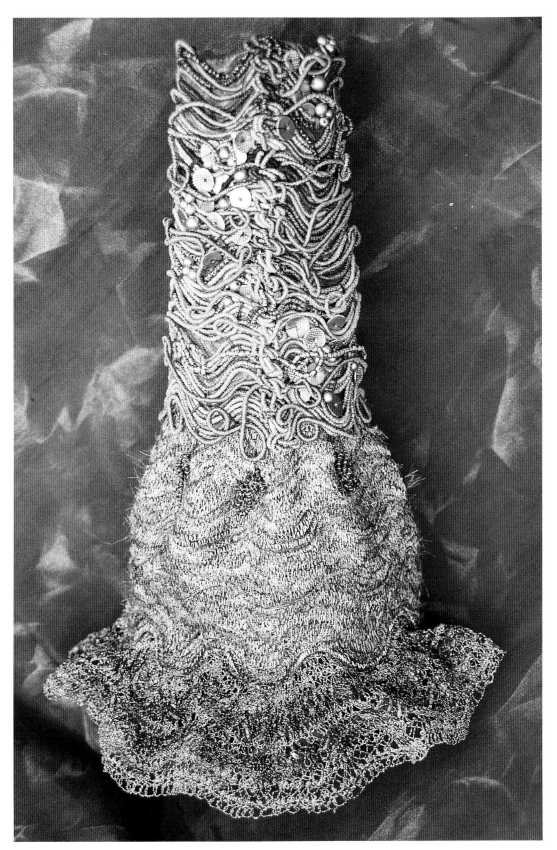

(Pages 88 and 89)
Beads trapped in pockets of fabric, among threads, between layers of fabrics, plastics and nets, and sequins trapped in machine-embroidered lace (boiled to remove the water-soluble fabric and distort the sequins)

The front of a gauntlet, combining machine embroidery with beads and fimo discs emerging from machine-wrapped cords (Ann Knights). The back of the gauntlet and a detail are shown overleaf

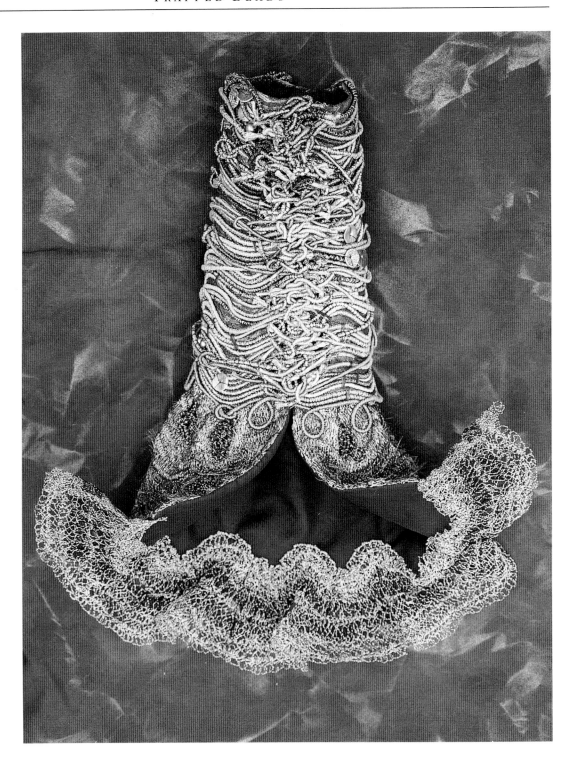

The back of the gauntlet

When attaching large sequins, jewels or *shisha* to fabric, the network of holding stitches sometimes appears too dominant. An alternative method is to lay pieces of translucent fabric or net over them, stitching round the shapes to secure them to the background fabric. Try using overlapped torn strips of fabric to give maximum colour interest.

The stitches may be unobtrusive running stitches, decorative stitches such as French knots, seeding or added beads. This stitching can then be seen from the design aspect, rather than just

The wrist section of the gauntlet, showing the machine-wrapped cords, beads and discs in more detail

from the functional need to attach the sequins or *shisha*. Scatter a few small beads on top of large sequins or *shisha* before covering with fabric.

As well as using bought translucent fabrics, make your own 'sheer' fabric by distorting muslin and scrim. Many of these can be made more open-weave by literally pulling them apart by hand, in a very crude form of a pulled-fabric technique. Free machining on muslin, using zigzag stitch, will produce a lovely open-mesh fabric which would show the gleam of the sequins and *shisha* underneath it.

SLITS AND FLAPS

Some thicker fabrics, such as handmade felt and pelmet vilene, may be slit sideways within their thickness with a sharp craft or Stanley knife. Do this very carefully, making a flap under which beads can be sewn, spilling out, as it were, on to the surrounding surface. On finer fabrics, these flaps are fragments caught in place with a few stitches, overlapped, and partly covering rich clusters of beads underneath.

BEADS UNDER STITCHES

Beads may be covered in whole or in part by embroidery stitches. It may be thought that the stitchery is usually worked first, with the beads sewn on afterwards. Reverse this process by sewing small beads, bugles or sequins over an area, then stitching freely on top of them, almost trying to ignore their presence. Free cross stitches, cretan, herringbone, buttonhole, fly and straight stitches can be worked by hand, and satin stitch or satin-stitch blobs worked carefully on the machine. As well as partly hiding the beads, this gives a raised appearance to the stitching. Combine applied torn strips of sheer fabric, silk nets and fine ribbons to this free stitching over beads to give a completely new look to the more usual ways of using beads with embroidery.

Strips of sheer fabrics are laid over massed beads, sequins and bugles, sewn to another fabric and secured with long stitches

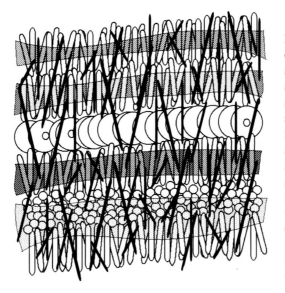

Paillettes and pieces of fabric trapped in pockets between net and transparent fabrics, with machine embroidery used to secure them (Carol Newman)

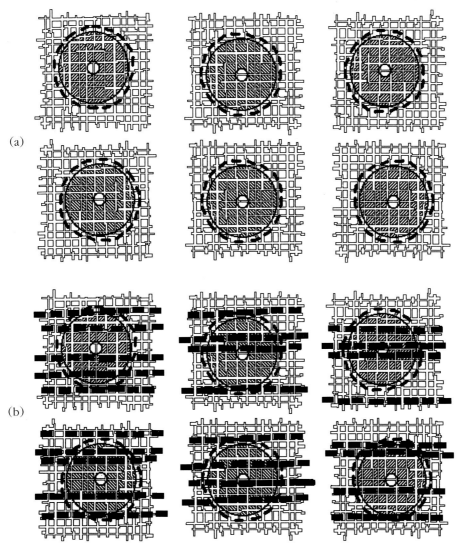

(a)

(b)

(a) Small pieces of scrim are placed over large sequins on a background fabric and secured with running stitches round the sequins
(b) A variation, in which narrow ribbons are threaded through the scrim before stitching

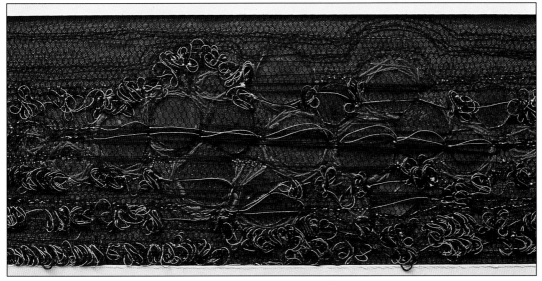

Shisha *trapped between black net and burnt orange silk, secured with machine stitching around and over them*

95

'Beads' made of fabric glued to straws, trapped under strips of mesh and couched threads, and embellished with small beads and pearls (Jacqueline Payne)

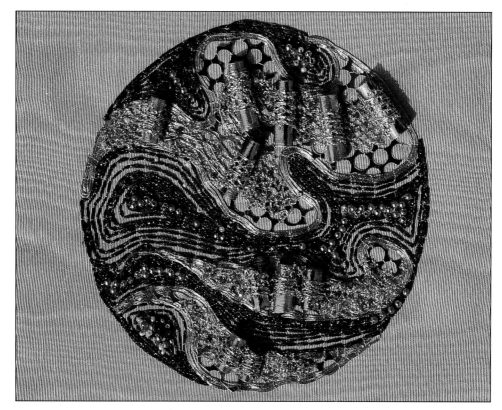

(Right)
Stitches over beads:
(a) massed beads are stitched to a fabric
(b) satin stitches are worked over some of the beads and then long stitches are laid over the top. These could be couched to give an undulating effect

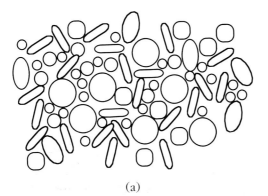

(a)

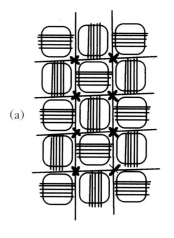

(a)

(Far right)
Stitches over beads:
(a) square beads, sewn to a fabric, are decorated with satin stitches which mould over the beads. A grid of laid threads is secured with cross stitch
(b) these beads are secured with overlapping diagonal stitches

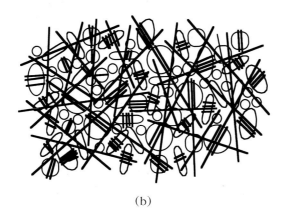

(b)

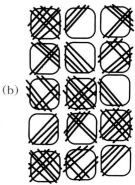

(b)

Bugles may be sewn to the fabric with satin stitch worked over them either by hand or machine. Completely cover the bugle or just part of it. This is an excellent way of attaching the extra-long bugles.

These techniques rely on the contrasts between shiny and matt beads, shiny and matt threads, padded and raised areas and the play of light on all the surfaces.

WRAPPED BEADS

Choose a medium-sized bead with a relatively large hole (many wooden beads are ideal for this). Using a fine thread, such as a rayon machine-embroidery thread, wrap the bead, over and over, going through the hole and over the side each time. Cover all or just part of the bead. Variegated metallic threads look particularly attractive when wrapped in this way, especially if the same thread is used for the embroidery itself. Sew the bead on to fabric in the usual way, or use in conjunction with cords, tassels or fastenings.

BEADS UNDER BEADS

This may seem a strange idea at first. Think of an area of small beads sewn on to fabric. Traditionally, perhaps, this would be considered complete. Add extra interest and texture by working over the top with long straight stitches threaded with more beads, worked as lazy stitch. Sew three or four rows of bugle beads side by side, adding threaded small round beads couched over the top of the rows at intervals.

One of us has bought a pair of shoes, heavily encrusted with beads and sequins which cover the entire surface (see page 34). On the sole of the shoe is written 'Too much is never enough', and perhaps that best sums up the feeling of this chapter.

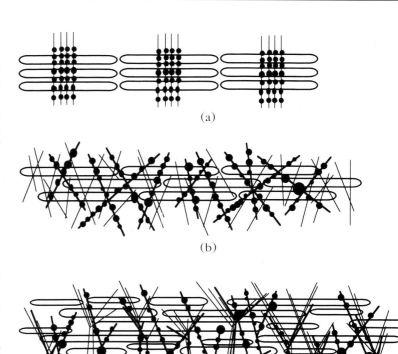

(a)

(b)

(c)

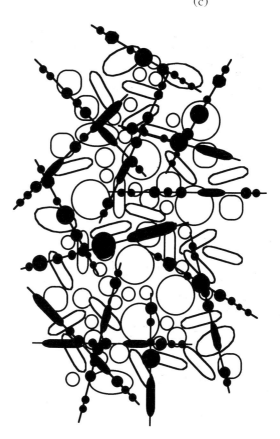

(Above)
*Beads over beads:
(a) long bugles are sewn to a fabric, and strung beads are couched over them
(b) long bugles sewn in a brick pattern are couched with random stitches and strung beads
(c) long bugles sewn randomly are decorated with fly stitch. Some of the stitches are strung with beads*

(Left)
An irregular mass of beads stitched to a fabric is further decorated with lines of strung beads, which can then move to and fro

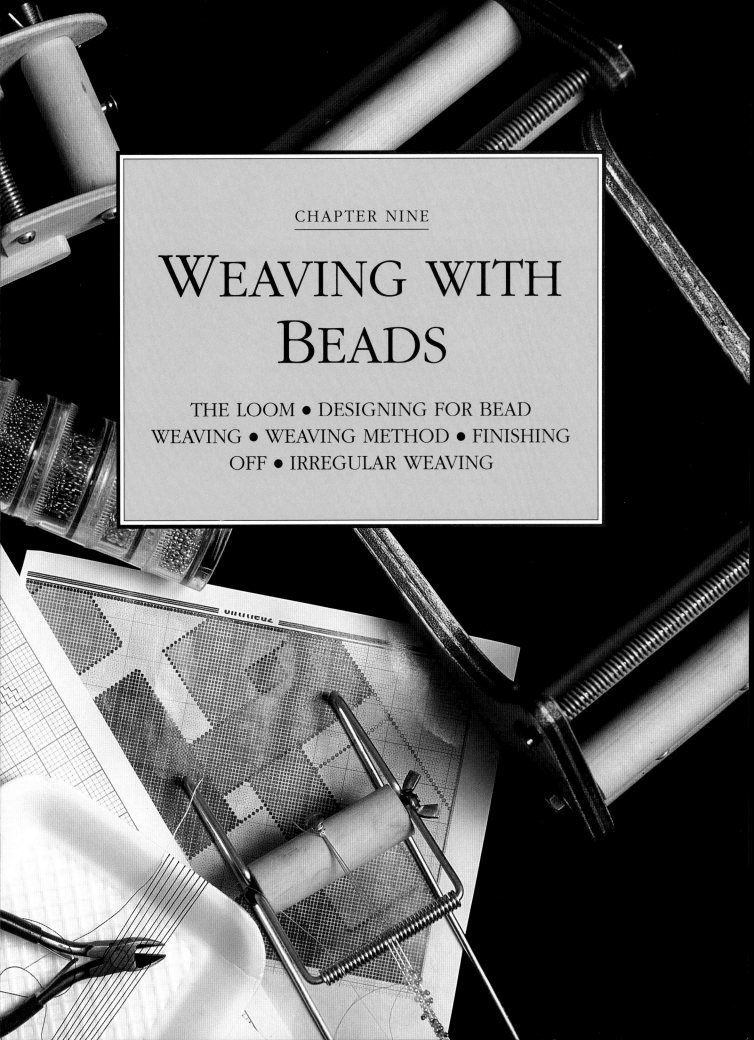

CHAPTER NINE

WEAVING WITH BEADS

THE LOOM • DESIGNING FOR BEAD
WEAVING • WEAVING METHOD • FINISHING
OFF • IRREGULAR WEAVING

Woven fabric has warp threads fastened lengthwise in the loom, with weft threads crossing from side to side and interlacing with the warp to make the fabric. Bead weaving is very similar, in that warp threads are held taut in the bead loom with the beads forming the weft. The result is unlike any other beading technique, with parallel rows of beads making a solid ribbon or fabric that is surprisingly strong and flexible.

Bead weaving, like other forms of bead embroidery, was very popular in Britain in the Victorian and Edwardian periods. Items made included chains, pin-cushions, panels or mirror backs and bags. The stocking (or miser) purse, a long tube of fabric carried by its middle, often had a central panel of cut-steel bead weaving. This helped to weigh down the two ends, even when no money had been inserted through the central slit.

North American Indians used bead weaving as a significant part of their ceremonial dress, with symbolic use of colour and design. The Zulus of Natal in South Africa also used bead weaving to celebrate special occasions, marking puberty, marriage and motherhood with the making of sashes, belts, aprons and veils. Belts, worn by a runner, were used to convey messages to other tribes. Bead weaving, worked with varying proportions of different colours, could even convey secret messages of love, as described on page 26. Today, these skills are aimed at the tourist rather than at their tribal heritage.

THE LOOM

Fairly inexpensive bead looms are available from many craft and hobby shops as well as from specialist suppliers (see page 127). They are relatively simple to make at home, giving you the advantage of being able to choose the length and shape to suit a particular purpose.

At the most basic level, for a first trial attempt, a polystyrene meat tray may be used, with the warp thread biting into the sides of the tray to keep it taut and in position. On a bought frame, wire springs or teeth hold the warp threads apart at certain intervals, corresponding to the width of the beads. Check that these threads will be held 5–7·5 cm (2–3 ins) above the base of the loom to enable your fingers to work easily beneath them.

Warping the loom

The warp thread must be strong. Choose a buttonhole thread or something more decorative, such as Jap gold or space-dyed silk twist. In general, you should use a colour a little darker than the beads. Warp threads can be different colours – alternate black and gold, for example – within the same piece of weaving.

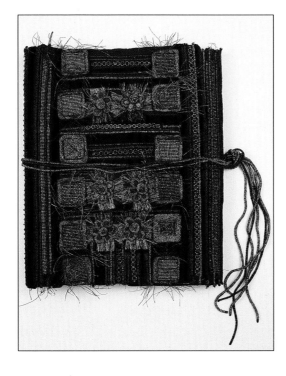

Embroidered book cover incorporating small squares and long strips of bead weaving using variegated metallic beads, blackberries, daisy chains and machine embroidery, built up in layers to give richness

The warp thread is continuous. Fasten it to the first pin or knob on the frame with a knot, winding back and forth through the gaps in the springs and the knobs at the other end. Make one more warp than there are beads in the design. Apply just enough tension to keep the threads taut (if the warp is too tight, the weaving will pucker when it is removed from the loom). Finish off by tying the thread to the last pin or knob. You may like to double the two outside warps for extra strength.

Sometimes the piece of weaving needs to be longer than the length of the loom. If this is the case, cut all the threads to the required length, plus an extra 25 cm (10 ins) at each end. Knot all the threads together at one end, slipping them over the knob on the roller. Pass the threads through the spaces in the springs, and hold them taut while you wind the excess length on to the roller. Tie the threads to the knobs on the second roller. Re-tighten the roller until the threads are held taut. The method varies slightly from model to model. If you are working in this way, weave the area that is visible on the warp threads. Loosen the rollers, and roll the finished part of the weaving round the roller nearest the start of the pattern, before tightening the rollers again. Then continue weaving on the empty threads.

Working on an extended warp can be rather difficult, so it may be easier to buy or make a loom of the required length so that you can see the whole pattern while you are working.

A chart designed on the computer for the side of a bag (both sides will be the same) on a board; magnetic strips hold it and show which line of the pattern is being worked from. Also shown is a bead loom warped with the start of the second side, and one completed bag side. The long warp threads are being used for the extra-long fringe

DESIGNING FOR BEAD WEAVING

Designs may be drawn out on a grid, but, as beads are not normally square, a design drawn on a square grid will be somewhat distorted when worked. Try plotting a grid on a computer, with the correct width-to-length ratio for a particular type of bead, and print it out on to acetate. Lay this over a freely painted design to see how it will translate into bead weaving. Books with charted patterns for knitting, cross stitch, canvaswork or weaving can all be used for bead weaving.

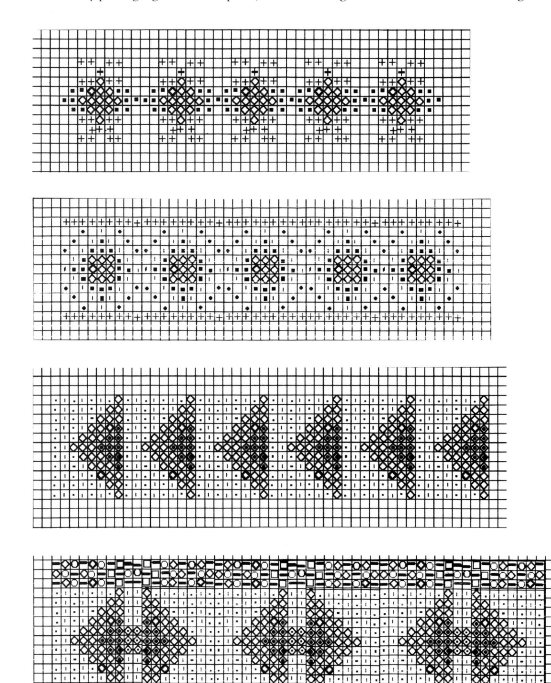

Four border patterns suitable for bead weaving

The front and back of a pieced and quilted silk bag, incorporating two different bead-weaving patterns, hand-rolled beads of silk and painted leather, and beaded tassels (Carol Dixon)

WEAVING METHOD

Choose beads of equal size for even weaving. Select the weft thread in a colour that complements the beads, bearing in mind that it will have to be threaded into a beading needle and to pass through each bead twice. If the beads are transparent, the colour of the weft thread will affect the colour of the beads quite strongly. Red thread through yellow beads, for example, will make them appear orange.

Start the weaving in the centre of the loom. Wax the thread and tie it on to the outside warp. Pick up the required number of beads for the first row (one less than the number of warps). Take the thread under the warps from left to right, pushing the beads up with your left forefinger, one in each space between the warps. Take the thread back over the warps from right to left, passing through the hole in every bead. If the weaving is too wide to take the needle through all the beads at once, pick up five or six beads at a time.

Before threading on the beads for the second row, wrap the weft thread round the outside warp thread, coming up from below between the first

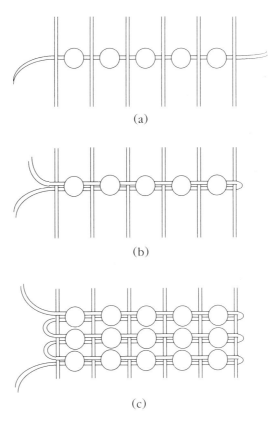

(a)

(b)

(c)

Bead weaving:
(a) the beads are strung and laid from left to right under and between the warp threads
(b) the beads are gently pushed up between the warp threads with a forefinger, and the needle threaded back through all the beads on top of the warp threads
(c) the weaving is continued in the same manner, with each thread passing through the beads twice, once below and once above the warp threads

(Right)
*A bead-woven
necklace, showing a
freer design and a
fringe worked on the
sides of the weaving.
Glass and silver-lined
beads are used, with
bugles added to the
fringe* (Joanne Bast)

and second thread. Then thread on the beads and
continue as before. The rows of beads should just
touch each other. Finish off the thread by tying it
to one of the inside warps and threading back
through a row of beads, before cutting it off close
to a bead. Neaten the start of the weaving by
undoing the knot in the thread, tying it to one of
the inside warps and threading back through a
row of beads before cutting it off.

The method of making shaped pieces of
weaving by increasing and decreasing is shown in
the diagrams below. Include one more warp or,
alternatively, one less warp with each row, as the
design demands. This will give a stepped appearance to a curve, as in counted cross stitch or
knitting patterns.

Slits within an area of weaving are worked by
weaving across the warps to the point where the
slit is required. Turn back, completing that side
for the necessary number of rows. Start a new
thread on the other side, working the same
number of rows.

*Decreasing is worked
by leaving out one or
more of the end warp
threads in each row*

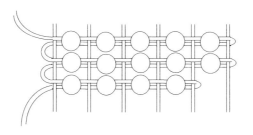

*Increasing is worked
by taking in one or
more warp threads in
each row*

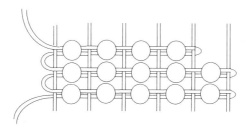

*Slits are worked by
using two threads, one
on each side of the slit.
The extra warp thread
is woven back through
the beads when the
work is taken off the
loom*

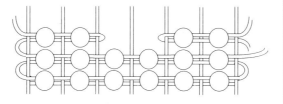

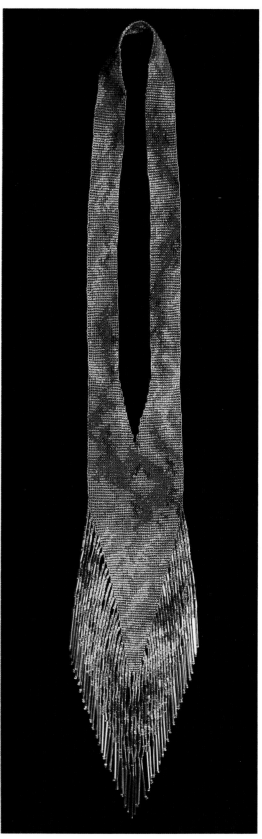

FINISHING OFF

When the weaving is finished, remove the piece from the loom by cutting the ends of the warp threads. If the weaving is to be applied, lay it on a firm backing fabric such as leather, or felt and fabric bonded together. Sew it to the background using stab stitches positioned regularly over the intersections of the warp and weft threads (this ensures that the weaving will be supported and remain flat). Then take the warp threads to the back of the fabric, tying them together in pairs.

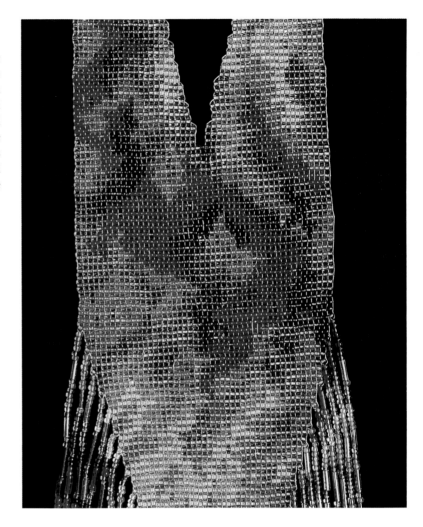

For many items, a fringed edge is more appropriate. Pin the weaving to a piece of polystyrene. Knot together each pair of warp threads, making an overhand knot right up to the edge of the beading. This is fairly easy if you insert a pin into the loop of the knot while it is still loose, sticking the pin into the polystyrene right next to the edge of the weaving. Then pull the ends of the thread to tighten the knot.

To make the fringe, put each warp thread in turn into a needle and pick up a number of beads. Having passed through the hole in the last bead, take the needle back through all the other beads, fastening off on the warp at the beginning of the weaving. Run the thread through some of the woven beads for extra security.

Fringes may also be worked on the sides of the weaving, even though there are no warp threads to use. See pages 110–13 for further information on this technique.

(Above)
A detail of the necklace opposite, showing the dividing and decreasing at the centre of the weaving
(Joanne Bast)

(Left)
Suggestions for a belt and two bags using lengths of bead weaving, beaded cords and tassels
(Christina Barry)

Small pieces of bead weaving may be joined together by matching the ends and tying the warp threads together in pairs. Weave the ends back into the weaving. You could make a feature of the join by adding loops or fringes of beads, or by covering the join in each row with a long bugle bead.

IRREGULAR WEAVING

Although beads of equal size are used for normal weaving, experiment with different-sized beads to give a lumpy and textured surface. Try, also, warping up the loom using only every third or fourth coil, leaving spaces between the warp threads. Weave in a random fashion, with different-sized beads, putting one, two, three or four beads between each warp thread. Push the rows into curves and waves, leaving spaces between them as you weave.

When you remove the weaving from the loom, do not knot the warp threads as usual, but leave them long. Place the weaving on a backing fabric and pin in place, adding hand or machine embroidery to secure it.

Regard a piece of bead weaving as a 'fabric' – a strong and flexible fabric. Sew more beads on top of it, paint it, weave textured threads or ribbons through it, or sew it to a fabric. The more ideas you try out, the more will undoubtedly come to you.

A Victorian bag using subtly coloured and cut-steel beads, woven on a bead loom (by permission of Judith Butt)

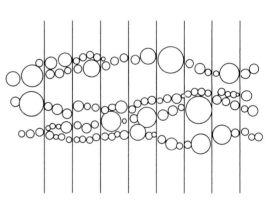

(Far right)
Irregular weaving: the spaces may be filled with woven threads or left empty

(a) Small beads may be added to the edges of the weaving to give a picot effect
(b) Fringes may be worked on the side of the weaving while the weaving is in progress, or added on afterwards using a separate thread

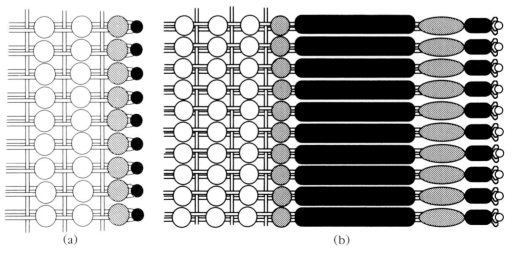

(a)   (b)

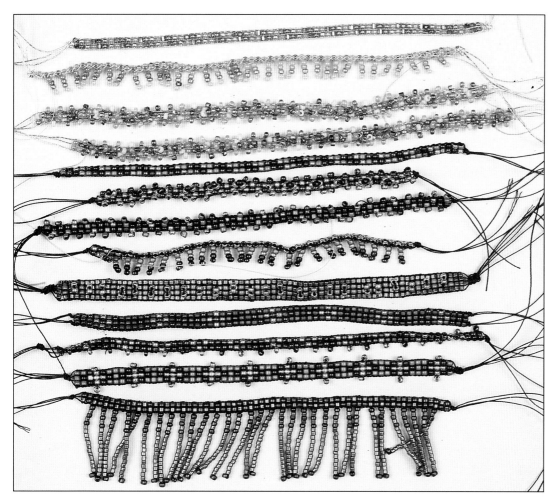

Woven braids, two and three beads wide. Some are plain weaving, contrasting matt beads with shiny metallic ones; one has a fringe worked on one side; and some have beads sewn to the edges (picots), or on top of the braids, or both. These extras are sewn on while the weaving is still on the loom, to take advantage of the taut tension

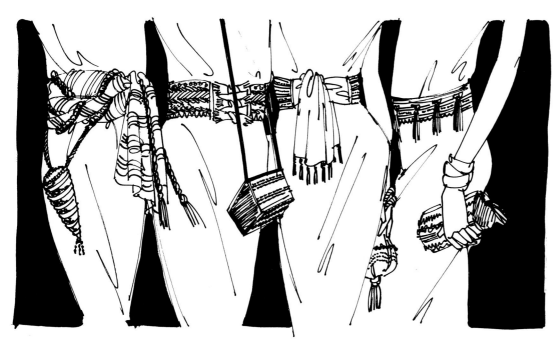

Suggestions for using narrow woven braids to decorate embroidered belts and bags. They could also be used on cuffs, collars, hats or worn as jewellery
(Christina Barry)

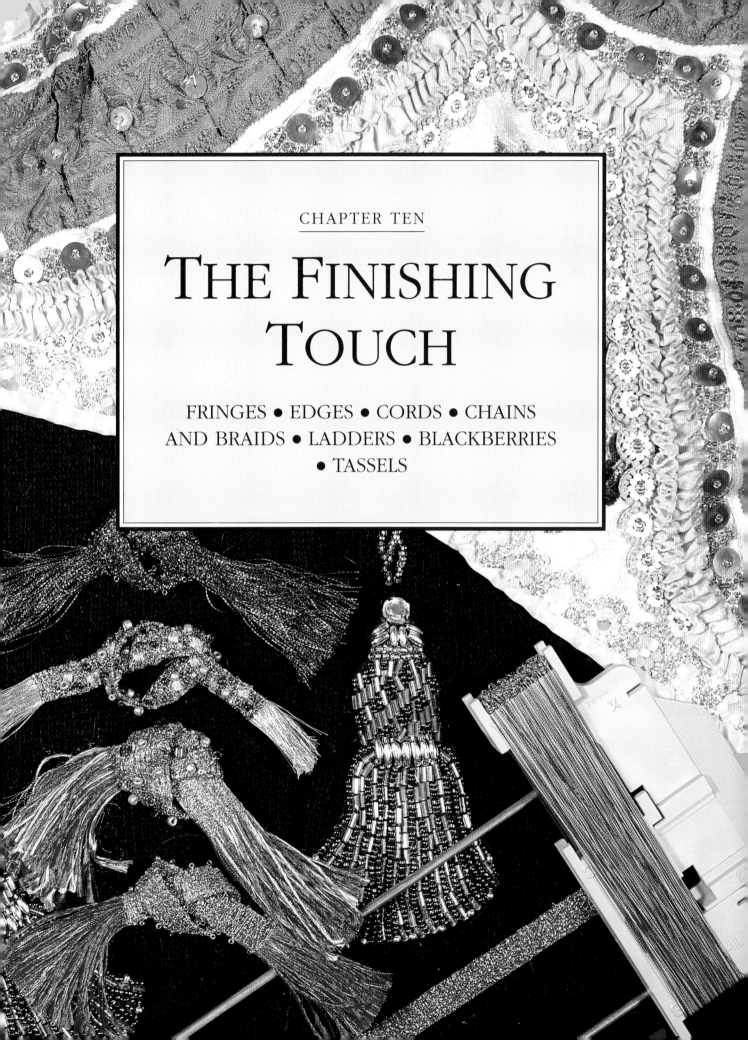

CHAPTER TEN

THE FINISHING TOUCH

FRINGES • EDGES • CORDS • CHAINS
AND BRAIDS • LADDERS • BLACKBERRIES
• TASSELS

Scalloped fringes:
(a) simple scalloped fringe
(b) bugles previously sewn on to the edge of the fabric set the size of the scallops
(c) overlapping scallops
(d) multiple scallops

Beads seem to be naturally associated with finishing techniques, whether for tassels, fringes, braids, cords or edgings on fabric. The exciting part is that there are so many possible variations on all these finishings, when you consider the size, colour, surface and types of beads, as well as the ways in which you can combine them.

We are including the techniques which we have found most effective and have enjoyed using. You may find variations in the methods of working in other publications, either historical or ethnic. We hope you will find your own favourites, using the ideas given here as inspiration.

FRINGES

There are as many different ways to make a fringe as there are items to embellish. It is usually presumed that a fringe is made on a fabric edge, but this is far too limiting. Decide whether you could add an area of fringing elsewhere, as a glorious focal point. Wherever the fringe is to be, consider the wear it will undergo, the weight and size of the beads and the method of working. These must all be appropriate for the article.

Looped and scalloped fringes

Although a simple beaded fringe may be worked directly on to fabric, it is often easier to work it on a length of braid, tape or ribbon, and to attach this after working the fringe.

Pin the braid on to a polystyrene block for stability while working. Thread a fine needle with a polyester or silk thread, running it through beeswax for extra strength, and work one or two backstitches into the edge. Thread on a number of beads or bugles in your chosen colours.

For a looped fringe, take the thread back into the fabric close to the starting point, working another backstitch. The distance between this and subsequent backstitches depends on the size of the beads used, and on how dense the fringe needs to be. The loops can be of equal or varying lengths.

For a more open single or double scalloped edging, mark or judge the distance required between the stitches in the fabric. This is not

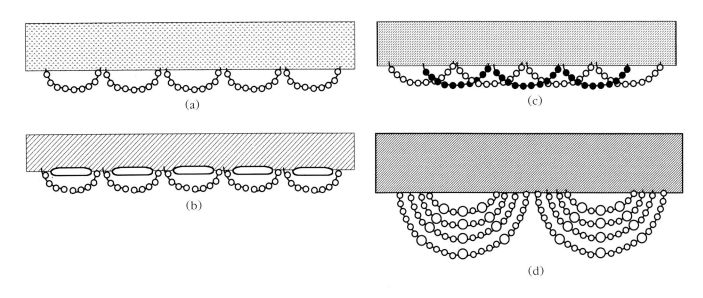

(a)

(b)

(c)

(d)

difficult if the same size and number of beads are used in each loop. An alternative method is first to sew on a row of bugles, parallel to the edge. The hanging loops of the scalloped fringe can then be placed between one, two or three bugles, thus keeping the spacing correct.

Many variations on this theme are possible. You could, for instance, fit loops and scallops one inside the other, going from small to large, overlap them sideways, or make 'V' shapes using bugles with a small round bead at the point.

Hanging strands

These may be made of round beads, bugles or a combination of both. Fasten the waxed thread securely on to the fabric. Pick up the required number of beads, miss the last bead and then take the needle back through all the beads above it. Take a small stitch in the fabric. Place subsequent strands along the edge, either all of the same length, or adding or subtracting a bead in each strand to give a shaped bottom edge.

A larger bead or pendant is often added at the end of the strands to give extra weight and movement to the fringe. When the last bead is large, however, the fringe will look neater if one small bead is added at the very bottom.

When using tiny beads for the fringe, the thread may be knotted at the bottom of each strand and sealed with a dab of clear nail varnish. Use this technique when the hole in the bead is too small to allow the needle and two threads to pass through it.

Hanging strands of beads may be used with scallops, either between them or added along the looped curve. Try a mixture of lattice patterns, using bugles, scallops and hanging strands together, for a really rich and elaborate fringe.

Patterned fringes

Intricate colour patterns and simple designs may be planned within an area of fringing. These are usually worked on top of a framed fabric on which the design is drawn. You may prefer to work the fringe attached to a tape, which is secured to a polystyrene board. Pin the paper design to the board before starting. For either method, the design can be counted from a chart, as shown in the photograph on page 113.

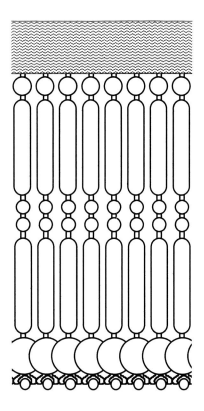

(Left and below)
Fringes of hanging strands, one with a straight bottom edge and one shaped

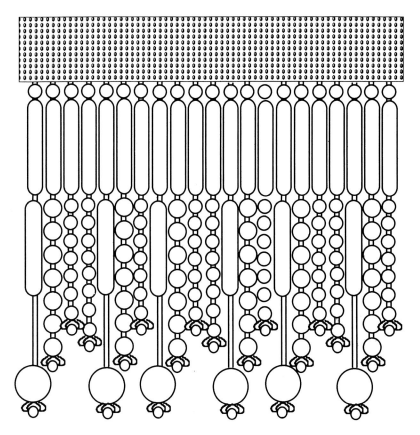

(Above)
*A fringe of long
hanging bugles on an
embroidered fabric
using couched gold
threads and purls*
(Cassie White)

*A fringe of copper and
bronze bugles and
beads, and crystal
beads, hanging from a
buttonhole edging*
(Jill Izzard)

Choose the beads according to the colours and scale of the design. Use a strong, waxed polyester or silk thread, making a knot and a backstitch in the fabric or tape. Thread on the beads to follow the design exactly, starting at the centre. Take the needle down into the fabric at the end of the line, making a few running stitches, and leaving a long length of thread. Continue in this way for all the lines of the design. If you are working on a board, the threads can be held in place at the bottom on a strip of double-sided sticky tape, which also prevents the beads from falling off.

When all the fringing is complete, take each thread in turn and put it into a needle. Missing out the last bead in each row, take the needle through all the beads above it and into the fabric or tape at the top, and fasten it off. If you have enough needles, these can be left in place on the threads, ready to be threaded back later when you are sure that the fringe pattern is correct.

Charted design suitable for a fringe with a shaped bottom edge

A chart and the fringe worked from it. To finish the fringe, the threads will be pulled out of their temporary holding place in the fabric, threaded back up through each strand of beads and finished off in the fabric at the head, which has been painted black. This will then be cut out and attached to another item

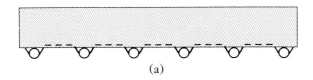

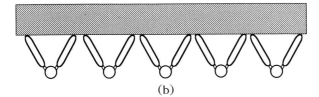

(a)

(b)

EDGES

Sewing beads on to the edge of a fabric, on ribbons or pleats, is more subtle than a fringe but, nevertheless, very effective. A broad cuff or shoulder panel on a shirt made with narrow, overlapping pleats edged with tiny pearls or beads, for example, would instantly transform an outfit.

It is easier and neater to sew beads on to a folded hem than on to a single layer of fabric. Run the needle through the fold, coming out to pick

(Above)
Beads sewn to the edge of a fabric:
(a) a simple edging showing separate beads with stitches hidden inside a fold
(b) bugles and beads making a different edge

Machine-embroidered ribbons, with beads sewn within the patterns and along the edges. Two ribbons have pleated or gathered ribbon attached to them, and one is an edging combining four ribbons, each one beaded

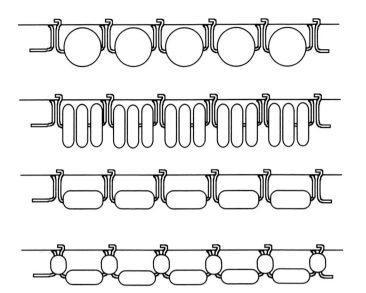

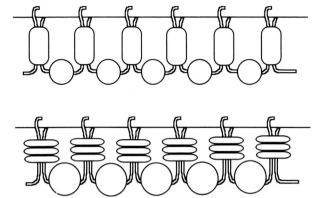

More complex edges and narrow fringes all worked on the edges of fabrics, embroidery, ribbons or quilting

up a bead, before making another stitch in the fold. A more elaborate version of this would be to work Armenian edging stitch, with two or three small beads on the thread between each of the knotted stitches into the fabric.

Ribbons are now available in a much wider variety of textures, colours and designs than ever before. Decorate these with rows of those little-used automatic sewing-machine patterns, before sewing beads or bugles along the edges. Work rows of decorative patterns on top of each other or add a narrow ribbon on to a wider one before stitching the two together. This will give more body to the ribbon, as well as encouraging it to twist and curl.

CORDS

Cords may be bought, made, hand- or machine-wrapped, dyed and, of course, embellished with beads. Cotton cord and string should always be boiled for five minutes to allow for shrinkage if used on an article which may be washed.

Look at your collection of different types of string and piping cords. Dyeing or space-dyeing a plain white cord is always a good starting point, especially if you intend to cover it with darker coloured threads and beads. Begin by using a medium-weight thread, wrapping round and round the cord, either covering it completely or in parts. String small beads on to a strong thread and wrap these round the cord. Make a feature of

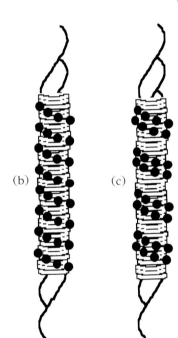

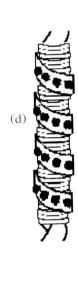

showing the wrapped threads underneath in parts – it is actually quite difficult to get the beads to cover the cord completely. To keep the beads in place, either make an occasional stitch through the cord or wrap tightly with just the thread in parts.

Wrapping with the finer machine-embroidery threads – especially the metallic type – looks very attractive with small beads added, either regularly or at random along the cord. Beads sewn on to narrow ribbon may be wrapped round a cord that has been previously dyed or hand-wrapped with threads.

(Above)
*Wrapped cords:
(a) a string or cord wrapped either by hand or machine
(b) threaded beads are then wrapped tightly over the top
(c) a different wrapping pattern
(d) the cord is wrapped with narrow ribbon previously stitched with beads*

Machine-wrapped cords

With a little practice, machine-wrapped beaded cords are easy to make and very versatile. They may be twisted, plaited and knotted, with the beads added either at the machining stage or by hand afterwards.

Thread your sewing machine with a fine machine-embroidery thread, select the zigzag stitch, remove the presser foot and lower the feed dog or teeth. Remember to lower the presser-foot lever to engage the top-tension system. Select a medium-weight string or thick wool. As a precaution, always hold the spool and bobbin threads when you first start to stitch (on some machines, these have a tendency to disappear down into the race when no fabric is used).

Hold the string between your thumb and first finger at the back of the machine, pressing it down on to the bed of the machine at the front with your other forefinger. As the machine stitches over the string from side to side, pull it very slowly away from you. This first covering of stitches is the basic machine-wrapped cord.

String small beads or bugles on to a long length of the same machine-embroidery thread. Starting again at the beginning of the cord, hold the strung beads and the wrapped cord together, while zigzagging over both. Machine fairly slowly to give the zigzag stitches time to slip between the beads, securing them in place on the cord. You could mass the beads in groups or place them more sparsely.

You may be anxious that the needle will hit a bead. In practice, should this happen, the bead is normally pushed out of the way by the needle. At worst, it is more likely that the bead will break than the needle. It is, however, a good idea to use a stronger needle than usual, such as a size 100 or even 110. Make sure that the width of the wrapped cord and the beads is narrower than the oval or rectangular hole in the base plate of your machine.

Twist, knot or plait a number of machine-wrapped, beaded cords to make a really rich cord for bag handles, jewellery, accessories or home furnishings. These would be wonderful, too, for adding to tassels.

A hat made from white silk which has been pintucked and embroidered, with burnt edges, machine-wrapped cords with tiny sequins couched to them, and hanging strands of threaded sequins (Joan Bowen)

Ribbon-yarn cords

Originally intended for knitting, ribbon yarn is a flat tube, resembling a narrow ribbon and reminiscent of childhood French knitting in construction. It is available in a wide range of colours, as well as metallic and random-dyed, and can be used as a base for many inventive cords.

String small beads on to a long thread and, placing these on top of the ribbon yarn, zigzag over both together, as described for machine-wrapped cords. You can make a fatter, rounded cord by first threading thick wool through the tube of yarn, using an elastic-threading bodkin. String small beads on to a long length of thread, and hold this together with the yarn while zigzagging by machine over both. Stitch densely

in parts and more openly in others, positioning the beads in random groups. You can make a more textured cord by threading thick wool into the ribbon yarn and gathering or ruching it up along the length. Add beads by hand or zigzag them in place by machine, so that they seem to nestle in the folds of the crinkly surface.

Use ribbon yarn to wrap round string or a piping cord. This can be worked with the ribbon yarn flat, with beads sewn by hand or machine along its centre. Again, you can make a fatter cord by stuffing the ribbon yarn with thick wool before using it to wrap a cord. Then string beads on to a long thread, wrapping these round the cord and slipping them into the valleys between the ribbon yarn.

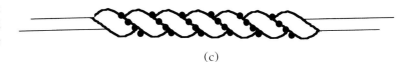

(a)

(b)

(c)

(Above)
Wrapped cords:
(a) machine-wrapped cord with strings of beads and bugles zigzagged on afterwards
(b) hand-wrapped cord with beads sewn on by hand
(c) stuffed knitting ribbon wrapped round a cord with a string of tiny beads wrapped round afterwards so that they sink into the valleys

Suggestions for beaded cords to be used as hair ornaments, and beaded tassels as earrings (Christina Barry)

We think that we have perfected methods of getting beads inside ribbon yarn. This gives a really lovely, weighted cord with the shine and shapes of the beads showing through. With some of the wider, loosely woven ribbon yarns, it is possible to push medium-sized beads, one by one, into the yarn (this only seems to work with oval beads, as the shape helps to open up the round end of the yarn). In between these beads, the ribbon yarn may be threaded through beads with large central holes – a little bit fiddly, but worth the effort if you have suitable beads.

It is much easier to push smaller beads down into the ribbon yarn using the following method. The main requirement is to get, and keep, the end of the flat yarn open. You will need a thin pencil or bodkin, a fat, plastic drinking straw or a fine metal tube, and a match. First seal the end of the yarn by touching it quickly into a flame, which helps to prevent its annoying habit of unravelling or

Various ways of stuffing beads into knitting ribbons using brass tubes and a pencil, or straws and a bodkin. When the ribbon is stuffed, the beads may be close together or pushed further apart, with thread wrapped between them or extra beads threaded or sewn on (beaded cord by Jean Hornsey)

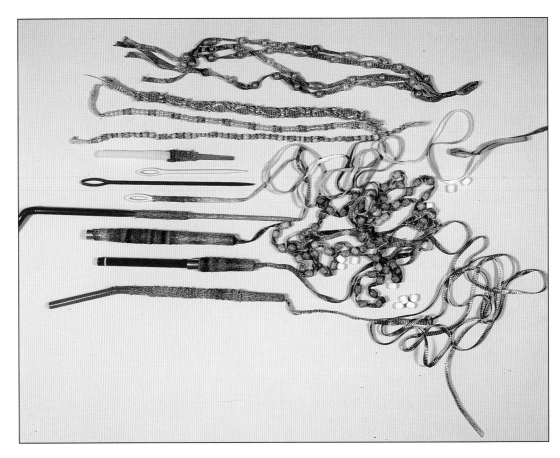

laddering. Insert the pencil or bodkin into the yarn, pushing it all the way through until it shows at the other end. Slip a short length of the straw on to this, pulling the ribbon yarn back on to the straw. Withdraw the pencil or bodkin.

(a)

Needle chains:
(a) a simple one-needle chain picking up four beads to make the loop
(b) this time six beads are picked up for the loop
(c) the chain turns into a braid when a second thread picks up a bead on the loop, alternating with extra beads

(b)

(c)

The end of the ribbon yarn is now held open by the straw, enabling you to put beads down it and into the yarn. You are obviously limited to a size of bead which will pass through the straw. If the beads stick, a little squeeze on the straw will propel them out, one by one. It really is great fun – rather like filling sausage skins. The resulting cord may be hand-wrapped with thread, passing between the enclosed beads, with extra beads added on the outside as well.

CHAINS AND BRAIDS

These make the most decorative edgings with all manner of possible variations and combinations. They are very easy to make and, with practice, the tension becomes easier to control for an even braid.

Needle chains

A simple chain is made by threading a needle with a strong, waxed thread, picking up a number of small beads (say three), followed by four large beads. Take the needle through the first of the large beads again, pulling the thread tight. Pick up three more small beads, then the four large beads and proceed as before, to make the required length.

You can make this chain wider by adding a second straight side to it. With a new thread, pick up three of the same small beads as before. Take the needle through the third large bead on the existing chain, add another three small beads, pass through the third of the large ones, and so on. Diagram (c) on the opposite page clearly shows this process. Vary the size and number of beads to alter the width and pattern of the chain.

Two-needle chains are made with two separate threads, each with a needle attached to the working end. Both threads go through each bead or bugle, one from left to right and the other from right to left, to ensure that the chain lies flat and does not twist. Any size or shape of bead with a central hole may be used for two-needle chains. For a braid, tie the ends together at one end, threading these back through the beads. Repeat at the other end. If you need a circular, continuous chain, tie the ends at one end to the ends at the other end. Thread through some beads to finish it off.

Daisy chains

A daisy chain is a familiar braid, either used on an edge or massed in rows applied to a background fabric. As with automatic machine patterns, it is a case of 'the more the better' with daisy chains.

Refer to the diagrams overleaf to help you with the sequence of threading. A simple daisy chain is made by threading three or more beads of one colour, traditionally the stem, then four beads of another colour (nos. 4, 5, 6 and 7). Pick up a slightly larger bead of a third colour (shown in black in the top diagram overleaf). Take the needle back through bead no. 4, pull tight, and thread on two more beads, nos. 9 and 10. Take the needle through bead no. 7 again and pull tight. It is important to keep the direction of the thread as shown in the diagram, so that the black bead ends up in the centre of the daisy. Repeat this sequence as many times as you wish. The central bead does need to be slightly larger than the other beads, or too much space will be left within the flower.

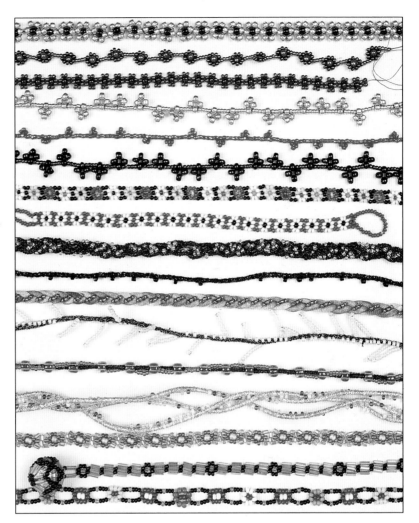

A more complex chain of continuous daisies can be made with eight beads plus a central one in each daisy. The thread goes twice round each block of four beads to hold the chain firm. The direction of threading changes within each daisy.

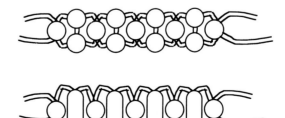

(Above)
Daisy chains from eastern Europe and Africa, one- and two-needle flower chains and machine-wrapped and hand-made beaded cords

Two-needle chains made by using two threads, one working from the right and one from the left, each passing through the central beads in opposite directions

A simple daisy chain. The beads are threaded on following the numbers in order, with the thread passing twice through beads nos. 4 and 7 in the direction indicated

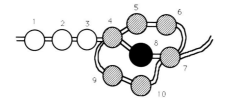

A more complex daisy chain

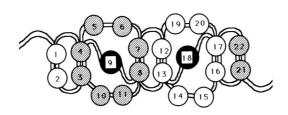

(Right)
Ladder made of bugles, with a fringe on one edge, worked afterwards

LADDERS

Wax a long length of thread, putting each of the ends into a needle. Unless the holes in the beads are quite large, use beading needles, as the holes will fill up as you work. Pick up two bugle beads with one of the needles, slipping these down to the centre of the thread. Take one of the needles and bring it back through the second bugle bead

in the opposite direction to the thread that already passes through it. Pull the thread tight. Add another bugle to one of the threads, passing the second needle through it in the opposite direction. Pull tight.

Continue in this manner until the ladder is as long as required, always passing the threads through the bugle beads towards each other. To finish the threads off, tie them together at the end of the ladder, threading back through the bugles. When adding a new thread, tie a length on to the

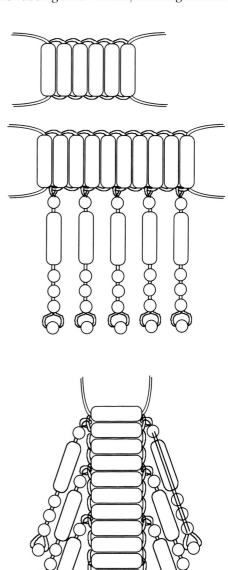

(Right)
Ladders made using two needles and threads and a varying number of beads and bugles

(Far right)
A fringe may be worked on both sides of a ladder

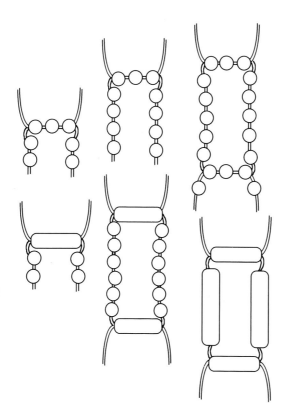

end of the used thread, running the ends through afterwards. As well as using only bugles for ladders, combine them with other beads, using enough round beads to measure the same length as the bugles. Alternatively, use round beads only (the number used together will depend on the size of the ladder required).

Ladders may be joined together to make wider braids. Hold two ladders next to each other, running a new thread through the top bugles in both ladders. Pass the needle back through the second row of bugles, then the third, and so on. When joining three or more ladders together, only pass through alternate rows of bugles for the

first join. To join a third or subsequent ladder, pass through the missed rows of bugles. The sides of ladders could be further decorated with hanging strands of beads or bugles, or any of the ideas described in fringing on pages 110–13.

BLACKBERRIES

These bead balls are useful for making flower centres or for adding to fringes and tassels. Using a strong thread, pick up three small beads and tie them tightly together with a knot. Adding one bead at a time, take the needle back through one

Machine-embroidered bag, finished with wrapped bead tassels (Joan Bowen)

(Above)
*Detail of the tassels
from the bag on the
previous page, showing
the small wooden
beads which have been
wrapped with metallic
machine-embroidery
thread* (Joan Bowen)

(Right)
*Detail of an Indian
bag showing cowrie
shells and pompons as
tassels*

tassel hang well with bounce and swing. Beads may be used on the cord, the head, round the neck, to form the skirt or on the ends of looped threads on a tassel.

Small-loop tassels

These little tassels make an ideal edging, worked over a cord or on to the edge or hem of a fabric. Cut a long length of fine silky or rayon thread, making a firm knot at the end. Using a beading needle, pick up a number of small beads on to the thread. Holding the cord against your finger, wrap the thread round it, not too tightly, dropping a bead off on the finger side each time. Count how many beads you use, so that you can repeat the tassel exactly. Withdraw your finger. Use the same thread to wrap the neck of the tassel securely, as closely as possible to the cord.

Tassels on the edge of fabric

Using a fine silky or rayon thread, fasten this on to the edge or hem of your fabric with a couple of neat backstitches. Pick up a small bead, wrap the thread loosely round your finger, then take a small

of the previous beads or through the centre of the mass to build up a ball. Depending on the size of the beads, you will need anything upward of twenty beads to make a blackberry. Work back and forth through the beads, adding new beads, and pulling tightly to mould the shape.

TASSELS

It seems appropriate to end the chapter with tassels – surely the ultimate finishing touch. Beaded tassels are even more special, with the beads, as always, adding shine and glamour. The weight of the beads makes even the simplest stitch in the fabric. Repeat until the tassel is thick enough, with a bead on every loop. Count the number of beads that you have used. Withdraw your finger, wrapping the neck of the tassel as closely as possible to the fabric edge.

Ribbon tassels

Narrow ribbons are widely available in a good colour range. Decide on the length of the tassel skirt, cutting pieces of ribbon to correspond with this measurement, and allowing a little extra for the head. Sew little beads or pearls on the lower third or half of each piece of ribbon. Hold the ends of the bundle of ribbon, together with the cord end, and bind tightly with strong cotton thread. Wrap more ribbon over the head to neaten it and make a nice, fat shape. The beads will add weight, as well as shine, to the ends of the ribbon.

Beaded-head tassels

Find a large wooden bead, a firm cotton-wool ball or a polystyrene ball. It is often necessary to make or enlarge the central hole. Cover whatever you use with a small circle of fine fabric, gathered up round the edge, pulled tight and fastened off. Alternatively, wrap with a narrow strip of very fine fabric or binding tape, threaded through the hole and going round the sides. Overlap it slightly to cover the head completely. Try to make this fabric covering as attractive as possible, as it may well show through the subsequent covering of beads.

Thread a beading needle and bring it up through the central hole. Pick up the required number of beads to make a vertical row from top to bottom of the head. Repeat this to complete four rows, spaced evenly, one in each quarter. Take a few stitches over the strung beads into the fabric covering to secure them in place. Continue filling each quarter with rows of beads until the head is covered. These can be packed very tightly or left a little more open to show the fabric beneath.

Beads can also be used to cover the head in a circular pattern, rather than vertical rows. Cover the head with fabric as described above. Pick up small beads on to a long length of thread, fastening this to the top of the head. Start to wrap the beads in a circular pattern. With a separate

needle and thread, go through two or three beads at a time, securing these to the fabric beneath. Continue wrapping a little and stitching a little, until you reach the base of the head. Fasten off both threads neatly.

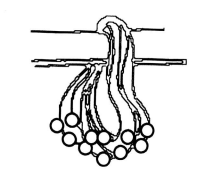

(Left)
Tassels worked on the edge of a fabric, or over a cord

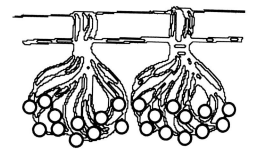

(Below)
Tassel made of beaded ribbons

(Left)
Tassel with a beaded head and another with a beaded skirt

Beaded-skirt tassels

The method used here is the same as for hanging strands of beads for fringing (see page 111). Select a strong thread, picking up a counted number of beads to give the correct length. Pass through the last bead in the strand and, missing it out, go back through all the others above it, to the top. Leave both thread ends. Repeat this for all the remaining strands. Put the two threads of each strand into a larger needle, and fasten them to the base of the covered head.

vertical rows of beads, which are secured with a separate thread to the base of threads underneath. A wrapped collar of beads round the neck would certainly brighten up an otherwise plain tassel, or could be added to any of the tassels already described.

Looped-head tassels

Cut a template from stiff card, twice the required length of the finished tassel, and cut out a central rectangle. Choose a fine rayon machine-

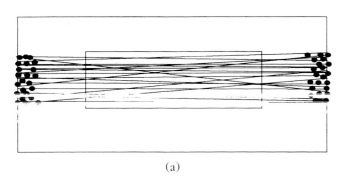

(a)

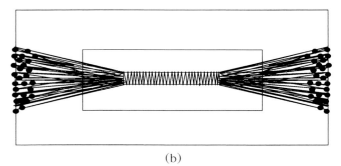

(b)

Thread tassels

Traditionally-made thread tassels can have beads added, either as an over-skirt, round the neck or over the head. An over-skirt of beads is made exactly as described for hanging strands (see page 111), these being fastened securely to the neck of the already made tassel. The head may be covered either with a circular pattern or with

embroidery thread, putting the end into a beading needle. Pick up approximately 120 small beads. Wrap the thread round and round the template, dropping off a bead at both ends. Although the threads are shown spaced out in the diagram above for clarity, try to keep them in a central bundle. Do not wrap too tightly or the template will bend like a boomerang.

When all the beads have been used, the central threads, over the cut-out rectangle, may be wrapped with the same, or a contrasting, thread. This can be worked by hand, or zigzagged on the machine.

To release the tassel, cut through the card template on one side. Ease the tassel off the card. Bend over the central wrapped portion to make a looped head, wrapping the two sides together to form the neck. The beads will fall to the bottom of each looped strand of thread, giving a most attractive tassel. The neck and looped head may be further embellished with beads sewn on by hand.

We hope that you will be encouraged to try your own variations of these finishing techniques, as well as deriving inspiration for every kind of embroidery with beads.

The finished machine-made tassel

Precious rose fan, using painted silk, richly embroidered by machine, with a machine-lace edging and antique beads and semi-precious stones, with an embroidered and beaded tassel head (Diana Dolman)

FURTHER READING

Some of the books in the following list are out of print, but may be obtained from your local library or from secondhand-book dealers who specialize in textile books. Their addresses are available from *Embroidery* magazine (see below).

Beads: Their Use by Upper Great Lakes Indians (Grand Rapids Public Museum)

Blakelock, Virginia L. *Those Bad, Bad Beads* (self-published, available from Spangles: see opposite page)

Carey, Margaret *Beads and Beadwork of East and South Africa* (Shire Ethnography, 1986)

Carey, Margaret *Beads and Beadwork of West and Central Africa* (Shire Ethnography, 1991)

Clabburn, Pamela *Beadwork* (Shire Ethnography, 1980)

Edwards, Joan *Bead-embroidered Dress* (Batsford)

Edwards, Joan *Bead Embroidery* (Lacis)

Fagg, William *Yoruba Beadwork* (Lund Humphries)

Fisher, Angela *Africa Adorned* (HarperCollins)

Giltsoff, Natalie *Fashion Bead Embroidery* (Batsford)

Goodhue, Horace *Indian Bead-weaving Patterns* (Bead-Craft, USA)

Johnson, Beryl *Advanced Embroidery Techniques* (Batsford)

Kliot, Jules and Kaethe *Beadwork* (Lacis)

Laye Andrew, H.E. *Batsford Encyclopaedia of Crafts* (Batsford)

Nicholas, Anwen and Teague, Daphne *Embroidery in Fashion* (Pitman)

Seyd, Mary *Introducing Beads* (Batsford)

Sherr Dubin, Lois *The History of Beads* (Thames & Hudson)

Smith, Monte *The Technique of North American Indian Beadwork* (Eagle's View Publishing Co.)

Thompson, Angela *Embroidery with Beads* (Batsford)

Weldon's Encyclopaedia of Needlework (Waverley)

White, Mary *How to do Beadwork* (Dover)

Embroidery magazine, published quarterly by the Embroiderers' Guild, PO Box 42B, East Molesey, Surrey KT8 9BB

Felt crosses secured with fly stitch, showing the contrast between clustered and spaced beads (Sarah Wiggs)

List of Suppliers

Bead Shop
21a Tower Street
Covent Garden
London WC2H 9NS
(Beads etc., storage boxes and pots, needles, threads, wire, looms, books)

Brighton Bead Shop
Department B
21 Sydney Street
Brighton
Sussex BN1 4EN
(Beads etc.)

Brodie & Middleton
68 Drury Lane
London WC2 0RX
(French bead varnish)

Janet Coles Beads
Perdiswell Cottage
Bilford Road
Worcester WR3 8QA
(Beads)

Craft Basics
9 Gillygate
York YO3 7EA
(Embroidery supplies, beads, looms)

Creative Beadcraft Ltd
Denmark Works
Sheepcote Dell Road
Beamond End
Amersham
Buckinghamshire HP7 0RX
(Beads etc., looms, threads)

Eastern Embroideries
7 White Swan
Monmouth NP25 3NY
(Semi-precious stones, freshwater pearls)

London Bead Company
339 Kentish Town Road
London NW5 2TJ

Necklace Makers' Workshop
259 Portobello Road
London W11 1LT
(Exotic and ethnic beads, threads, beaded articles)

E. Ploton (Sundries) Ltd
273 Archway Road
London N6 5AA
(Gold and silver transfer leaf)

Spangles
1 Casburn Lane
Burwell
Cambridgeshire CB5 0ED
(Beads, wire, needles, tubes, books)

Useful Adresses

The Bead Society
Carole Morris (Secretary)
1 Casburn Lane
Burwell
Cambridgeshire CB5 0ED
(Send s.a.e. for details)

The Embroiderers' Guild
Apartment 41
Hampton Court Palace
East Molesey
Surrey KT8 9AU
(Collection of embroidery with heads)

Museum of Mankind
Burlington Gardens
London W1
(Collection of ethnic beading)

Victoria and Albert Museum
Brompton Road
London SW7 2RL
(Collection of beaded items)

INDEX